The Journey

An Autobiography

Dr. Ken Blue

PREFACE & DEDICATION

Several of our church members suggested that I put in print some of the events of my journey from childhood to the present. At first, I was reluctant at the thought of writing about my life. There just seemed to me a thought of vanity and self-promotion to consider such a task about self. However, after much thought and prayer, I decided that writing the journey of God's grace to me, and how He dispensed that grace might be of interest and encouragement to my family and to others who may read it.

Every person has his or her story or journey to tell. No one understands your story better than you. I am sure, like my journey, yours has had valleys, hills, crooks and turns. Nevertheless, I have discovered, as you will upon reflection, that those hills and valleys were all a part of God's perfect plan.

As I ponder my childhood, precious memories of my mother and the impression she made on my life will become evident to the reader as he too follows the journey. I have attempted to draw from childhood memories, of those who come to mind and had an impact on my life to make this journey what it has become.

I dedicate this book to Joyce, my loving wife of over 60 years, and co-laborer in every aspect of our ministry. In addition, I have written with each of our five children in mind. They are Rocky, Randy,

David, Steve, and Lisa. My one grief is the sacrifice they endured through my college years, and the years my focus was too much on the ministry. Lastly, I dedicate it to the members of Open Door Baptist Church, whose love and encouragement sustained our family through forty years of the journey.

CONTENTS

FORWARD BY DR. JASON MURPHY

Pastor of Open Door Baptist Church

Lynnwood, WA.

Over 40 years ago, God brought a young country boy from the Ozark Mountains in Arkansas to Lynnwood, Washington, a bustling suburb of the Seattle metropolis. He and his wife, Joyce, came to the great state of Washington where he founded and faithfully pastored the Open Door Baptist Church for 39 years. Pastor Blue began knocking on doors in the neighborhood, with a desire to plant a church and reach people with the gospel.

The first service held at Open Door Baptist Church was in the Blue's living room, October 1969. With chairs set and hymnals in place, they waited patiently to see who would come. The first official recorded attendance for this new church would show that Pastor and his family were the only ones present for this inaugural service.

So, what did Pastor Blue do? He held a Sunday evening service, and, lo and behold, Jean Wake, a Christian lady, looking for a church home would find her way to that evening service hosted in Pastor's home.

Where many would have quit or given up, Pastor Blue determined to remain faithful to where God had called him, and over the next 39 years. This faithfulness and determination would prove to be a hallmark of his ministry.

Since those humble beginnings, Pastor Blue has impacted countless lives over four decades of ministry. He would see Open Door grow to hundreds enrolled in weekly attendance, reach scores of families with the gospel, and trained dozens of men who are faithfully serving the Lord in full-time ministry across the globe.

Dr. Blue, Pastor emeritus, is a faithful pastor and still is a tremendous example to so many. He has written dozens of helpful commentaries and continues to minister to people today through his writings. He holds degrees in Bachelor of Religious Education, Doctor of Divinity, Doctor of Theological Studies, Master of Biblical Studies, and a Doctor of Ministries.

I am confident you will be blessed and inspired as you read this book and discover the journey God continues through the life of a little boy from Boswell, Arkansas. The book describes in vivid detail the seemingly insurmountable circumstances God brought Pastor Blue through. I am also confident that this book will be a blessing to all those who read it.

Thank you, Pastor and Mrs. Blue for your example.
Dr. Jason Murphy, Sr. Pastor

1
IN THE BEGINNING

The beginning for me was July 20, 1938, in the Ozark Mountains in Izard County, north central Arkansas. I was born in a one-room cabin and delivered by a midwife by the name of Mrs. Pete Lane, and named Kenneth Joe Byler. A birth certificate was not secured. My mother was divorced at that time and retained her maiden name. Before I acquired my driver's license, I wanted to take the name of my stepfather. I liked the name "Blue." My mother wrote the courthouse in Izard County and requested a copy. The place for the father was left blank since my mother had refused to expose my biological father. Thus, Byler was my last name. That was the name I used until I had it changed. The change was not a legal adoption, but a legal name change. It was a very simple matter.

2
MY GRANDPA AND GRANDMA BYLER

Most of the houses in the county were unpainted. However, Grandpa's house was a brilliant white and it was beautiful. Thus, we called it the "white house." The house had a front porch and a porch swing. We enjoyed sitting out at night and watching the lighten bugs and wondering at the shooting stars.

The house was midway between the small town of Boswell, and the city of Melbourne, on Jumbo Road. Melbourne is the county seat of Izard County, and when you lived in the country, Melbourne appeared to be a large city to a small boy. The population of Melbourne in 2009 was 1,682. Boswell had about one hundred residents when I was a child. The road between these two towns was a rough dirt road. Much of the road consisted of flat rock. It was common to see rocks the size of a grapefruit that the road grader had pushed to one side as he graded it.

The road was a W.P.A. project (Works Project Administration). It was set up under FDR's New Deal. Its purpose was to put the millions of unemployed Americans back to work through government projects. These involved rebuilding the American infrastructure such as highways, bridges, parks, etc.

When we rode in the iron-wheeled wagon to either town, we needed to have dental work when we arrived, and our rear end readjusted when we returned home.

On many occasions, mom and I would walk the dusty rock-strewn road to Boswell or to Melbourne. I enjoyed the walk with her. She would talk to me and sing gospel songs. My mother's voice was angelic to me. Now and then I would see a glade lizard or a snake which would distract me. I looked for just the right size rocks to throw at them. Glade lizards would chase you. Believe me, I ran from them, ignoring all the rocks. One particular walk with my mother, to the peach orchard located several hundred yards west of grandpa's house, stands out in my memory. There, between the orchard and the white house, my mother pointed to the place where the house, in which I was born, had stood. The only thing remaining was an empty dry pond.

A thicket of small oak trees surrounding Grandpa's house on three sides provided a great place to play "Cowboys and Indians", or a game of "hide-and-seek". A huge oak tree stood beside the road, with limbs extending over a sand bed in the road. The adults had tied a rope to one of the limbs. An old automobile tire was attached to the rope and it made a perfect swing for me and my two cousins, Johnny Wayne and Jimmy Dale. Johnny Wayne was about a year older than me. He had straight black hair and dark complexion. There was Indian blood in our family. Jimmy Dale was about two years younger than me. I did not have brothers or sisters, so Johnny and Jimmy filled that void. We were as close as a brother could be. Some of my best memories include Johnny and Jimmy.

We didn't have electricity or running water at the white house. An old fashion coal oil lamp provided the light. You were able to read if you were only inches away. It was necessary to carry it from room to room to have light. When the wick burned to an uneven condition, it caused dark smoke to come from the high side of the wick and covered the inside of the globe with soot. Mom would take a newspaper, crumple it, and stuff it inside the globe. She turned the paper inside the globe removing the soot, and the globe was like new again.

Sometime later, Grandpa upgraded to a new and better lamp. It too burnt coal oil, but instead of a wick, it had a mantel like the modern day Colman Lanterns. The mantels were very fragile. The task was to move the lamp with caution from room to room without damaging the mantel. We were amazed at the amount of light it put out. You could see all the way across the room with the new lamp!

Drinking water was from a spring that was about a quarter mile from the house. The crystal clear water bubbled out of the ground, and was so cold it made your teeth ache. The spring was also where mom washed our clothes. She filled an iron kettle with water and built a fire under it. She dipped the boiling water into a washtub, and with a washboard and lye soap, she did the washing by hand. Afterward, she rinsed them in clear water, wrung them out by hand, and carried them back to the house, where she hung them on a close line to dry. At other times, she hung them on branches by the spring.

Wooden rain barrels located at the back corners of the house collected rain water from the gutters. I believe that water was used to bathe and to wash dishes. I don't remember us using it for drinking water, although I did taste it once. It tasted awful, like the wooden staves of the barrel.

We didn't have an outhouse, so everyone went across the road to take care of business. A Sears Catalogue was usually available. If not, a stick or leaves would do. Enough about this, I'm sure that's more information than anyone wanted. However, these are my earliest memories, and they were all good.

Other than the Lone Ranger, Grampa was my hero. I did not have a dad, so Grandpa was a male influence in my early years. He was over six feet tall, and did not have an inch of fat on him. The hard work had made him as hard as steel. He had light brown wavy hair. He was part German and Irish. Music came naturally to him. He could not read a note, but he played the five-string banjo, the French harp, the Jews harp, and the fiddle.

I remember seeing him sitting and reading the Bible. That made a great impression on me. I will forever be grateful for his kindness. My mother told me of a time when I bumped my head on something and came crying to her. Grandpa was nearby, and said, "Son you will get lots of bumps in life, but not if Grandpa can help it." That story meant much to me and let me know how much he loved me. He never said a cross word to me. You can understand why I loved him so much.

Grandma was the greatest lady I ever met. She was quiet and proper. She had respect for the men folks and herself. The last time I spoke with her, I asked when she got saved. She said, at the age of eighteen. Grandma was half Cherokee Indian. She looked the part and was beautiful. I remember watching her comb her long black hair that hung to her hips. I always wondered how she managed to get all that hair arranged on her head. Grandma lived to be one hundred and one day. I don't remember her ever being sick. Her heart just wore out. Grandma was the idol of all her grandchildren and we loved her very much.

Grampa had a large battery operated radio. Just like anything else, the battery would run out of power after a few hours. That is why we had to conserve and only listen to the important programs. The news was important to Grampa. The Lone Ranger was bigger than life to me, and I had most of the episodes memorized by heart. On Saturday night the entire family would gather round that old radio and listen to the Grand Old Opry. Thanks to Grandpa, I grew up on the Lone Ranger and country music.

Although we were dirt poor, Grandpa managed to buy a used car. I don't know if it was a Model A or Model T. It had four doors, and was black. I believe Henry Ford said, "You can have any color you want just as long as it is black." Below the radiator, just above the front bumper was a hole where you inserted a crank to start the engine. The story is that Grandpa wrecked the car, and since he had little or no money, that was that.

3
WORLD WAR II AND
THE GREAT DEPRESSION

In those days, World War II was winding down, and the Depression was coming to an end. I have sketchy memories of those days. Government stamps were necessary to purchase many items. Some things hard to get were coffee, gasoline, tires, and sugar. I am confident many other *commodities* were scarce, but I can't remember what they were. Coffee was impossible to buy during those years. Mom told of how they would parch corn meal on the stove, and then strain hot water through it. That was their coffee. Flour and water were all the had to make their biscuits and gravy. I was too young to understand how difficult those days were for adults with families.

Mom told how Grandpa would take biscuits and gravy to work with him on the railroad, and they would be frozen solid by lunch time. My mother would tell that story with tears in her eyes. Only those who went through the depression know the heartache and difficulties of those days.

The war and the depression had taken a toll on America, and it took a tragic toll on Grampa. It took several years to recover from the loss and heartache, if he ever did. Grandpa and Grandma had eight children. My mother, Flora, was the oldest. She was born May 16, 1909. The names of the other children were John, Louise, Clarence, Pearl, Floyd, Lloyd, and Lucile. Grampa's four sons were all drafted into the army. I believe Uncle John remained stateside. Clarence went to Germany, where he drove a Halftrack. Eisenhower was president at the time, and a smart uniform jacket was called the "Ike jacket." Uncle Clarence gave it to me, and I wore it with pride. The twins, Floyd and Lloyd, were sent to the Philippines; both died a month apart. Grandpa never was the same after the loss of his twin boys. They were only 20 years old. He became angry and began to drink. He wanted to kill every "Jap" he saw.

I was about five years old at that time; I remember seeing the women folks crying. My aunt Lucile was lying across the bed crying. I did not understand what was wrong, so I asked her. She cradled me in her arms and told me, Floyd was killed. Lloyd wrote home and said that Floyd had died in his arms with a bullet through his head. One month later the family was notified that Lloyd was "missing in action." They never found his body. That story has more of an emotional impact on me today than it did then.

4
MAKING MOLASSES

Uncle John Byler, my mother's younger brother, lived about half a mile east of the white house. One event that has stayed with me throughout the years was watching the family make molasses. Uncle John had a sugarcane field next to the dirt road. They set up the process next to the road. They dug a pit for the fire. It was about fifteen feet long, three feet wide, and about a foot deep. A shallow pan was made of sheet metal to fit over the pit. A horse was attached to a pole, and the other end was attached to some gears that ground the sugar cane fed into the gears. The sap ran out into a bucket, and then poured into the pan. The fire cooked the sap. It thickened and turned brown as it heated. A couple of long poles with a short two-by-four nailed to the other end of the pole worked as ladles. These were used to move the juice back and forth until the right texture was just right. Now you know the process of making homemade molasses.

5
MURDER AND THE MANHUNT

Grandpa's brother, Jim Byler, lived about four miles east of the white house on the Jumbo Road. His was a small, typical, unpainted house like many you find in the Ozark Mountains. Uncle Jim, as we called him, had a wife and four children.

The name of Uncle Jim's oldest son was Rupert. I have some sketchy memories of Uncle Jim and his family. I was only six years old when the following drama unfolded. It all began on a Tuesday, December 4th at 2:30 P.M. 1945. The story, as I recall it, was that Rubert could not read or write and he had some minor problems with the law.

Izard County was, and still is, a dry county. That is, you had to go to other counties to buy liquor unless you were lucky enough to know a moonshiner, and there were plenty of them in the hills. However, Rubert was the perfect person for the following scheme.

The courthouse and county seat for Izard County were in Melbourne. County and city officials had Rubert going to other counties that were not dry and load his car with liquor and bringing it back to the Court House in Melbourne. (Perhaps Rubert was paid with plenty of whisky.) County and city officials would have their parties in the Court House basement. There was much corruption in the city and county government. The good citizens of Izard had no idea of the corruption in their city and county leaders. They were about to find out.

Across the street from the Court House was a car dealership that sold new and used cars. Rubert bought a used car that was fast and perfect for his assigned task. However, unknown to Rubert, or the citizens of the county, many of the used cars were stolen. They were brought to Melbourne from Missouri, chopped, repainted, and sold to the public. Rubert had purchased one of these stolen cars. It was a 1937 Ford, V-8, two door sedan. There were few cars in Izard County that could outrun the V-8 Ford. It was the "bootleggers" dream.

On one run, with a load of illegal alcohol, Rubert wrecked his car, and it and the liquor went up in flames. All that remained of the car was the frame. A state patrolman ran the number on the frame and discovered that the car was stolen in Michigan.

The boys at the Court House, along with the dealership were very nervous. Serious action had to take place before Rubert had a chance to talk.

6
THE PLOT TO KILL RUBERT BYLER

On a set day, two county sheriffs had a plan. They would arrest Rubert, on the charge of writing hot checks (Rubert could not read or write). Their story would be that they shot him for trying to escape. That would be their account of events; problem solved.

They parked the police car about a ½ mile down the dirt road and out of sight of the Byler house. The officers entered the porch and knocked on the door. Rubert, his wife, and parents were home. The officers told him they had come to arrest him, and they put handcuffs on him. Rubert sensed that this was a setup and began to struggle with the officers. He was able to get his hands out of the cuffs, and by this time, his wife was at the door with a shotgun. Some say it was the wife who shot the sheriff and not Rubert. Officer James Lawrence Harber was shot and killed, as the other sheriff retreated to the woods and made his way back to the parked police car.

Rubert and his wife were on the run for six months, which launched one of the largest manhunts in Arkansas history. The posse was a drunken mob according to testimonies. The hunt was on for Rubert and his new wife. When the posse came to the house the next day and found the dead officer, they began killing every animal Uncle Jim owned. They also burned the house to the ground. Although I was young, I remember seeing what remained of the house. There was nothing but ashes. The story is, the dogs had eaten on the body of the dead officer. The posse, or mob, was infuriated and vowed to kill Rubert and his wife on site.

Rubert and his wife hid in caves, in creek bottoms and underbrush. He told my Grandpa, at times they could have reached out and touch members of the posse. They ate berries, leaves, and bark from trees to stay alive.

On one occasion, mom and I were walking to Boswell. She was carrying a gallon tin pail. I remember it was a yellow lard bucket. (Lard was made from pig fat and refined for cooking). A few miles from our house, mom said she had to go to the bathroom. I waited on the road until she returned. I noticed she did not have the bucket. I ask about it, and she told me not to worry about it. I know now it had food that she left for Rubert.

Armed men were everywhere. From the kitchen window, I could see a man behind an old rusty car body. It was about fifty yards from the house. He was watching, and waiting with a rifle in hand. Orders had been given to shoot Rubert on site.

One night some of the posse came in Grandpa's house searching for Rubert. Everyone was in bed. The posse went from room to room and shined a flashlight in every face. They were concerned when they saw a face that they did not recognize. Grandpa explained that this was his second son. Clarence was on leave from the war in Germany.

The manhunt had lasted several months. My Grandpa made contact with Rubert and told him both he and his wife faced death if they did not turn themselves in, Rubert agreed on one condition. He would not turn himself into authorities in Melbourne. Under cover of darkness, Grandpa took Rubert and his wife to the city of Batesville where he surrendered.

Later, Rubert was brought back to Melbourne to face his trial. It was the spring of 1946. I remember the courthouse was packed. Rubert was found guilty and given the death sentence, which was to be the electric chair within the next six months.

However, few knew that the judge, the prosecutor, the sheriffs, and witness were related. Not only did the corruption of the county and city officials come to light, but an appeal to the supreme court of Arkansas was secured. There would be a new trial. Rubert's new sentence was twenty-one years in prison with the possibility of parole. I am not sure, but I believe he served six years. Rubert lived the rest of his life without incident. He died in California.

The documented evidence of this event is in the excellent book by Bill Dwayne Blevins, Eds. The title of the book is Rubert. He had 1000 copies printed. I have a copy 467 signed by the author.

7
CANCER AND THE BYLER FAMILY

Cancer plagued the Byler family. Grandpa Byler died of stomach cancer. Both John and Clarence died of cancer. Uncle John died of lung cancer. Aunt Louise avoided cancer. She had a stroke. Clarence died of melanoma on his leg. Aunt Pearl lost an eye to cancer. My mother had major breast cancer, but by the grace of God she survived to live until she was age 92. Cousin Johnny Byler died in his early thirties of Leukemia. Cousin Burl Pierce died at age 46 of testicular cancer. I had major colon cancer at age 31. By God's grace, I have been cancer free for over forty years.

8
MOTHER MOVING FOR WORK

My mother moved wherever she could find work. One of the moves was to a small community called Lunenburg. It was much smaller than Boswell and we lived with my Uncle, Troy Craig. He was married to Mom's sister aunt Pearl. Uncle Troy was not a tall man, and he had lost most of his hair and his teeth. I never saw him wear anything except bibbed overalls. The bib had a small pocket where he slid his pocket watch that was attached to a small chain. It also had a larger pocket where he placed his false teeth. I don't remember ever seeing him wearing his teeth. Although I was young, I remember how kind he was to me.

He was an expert at making windmills, whistles, and all kinds of toys carved from wood. Whittling and talking was a well-established pastime in Arkansas.

It was at his house; I remember my first Christmas. He would hang socks behind the wood stove. On Christmas morning there would be nuts, candy an apple or an orange in each sock. Santa has visited us that night!

Uncle Troy grew peanuts and took me to the field to help pull them. We stored them in the loft of the barn to dry. He let me ride on one of his horses across the creek. I remember that I was afraid the horse would lay down in the water. He assured me that that would not happen and said I talked so much; he gave me the name, "Windy

Joe." I am thankful that we lived in Lunenburg with Uncle Troy. He was always kind to me, and I loved him for that.

Later they had moved to Boswell across the lane from Grandpa's house. Years later, his wife, Pearl, was in the nursing home in Calico Rock. She passed away there. I sat on the porch with Uncle Troy, and we talked about the past and watched the dozens of hummingbirds suck up the nectar from the feeders he hung on the porch. That was my last visit with him. Later he had surgery and died on the operating table. I loved him very much.

During the depression, my mother took odd jobs house cleaning or any other work she could find. We lived with the people for who she worked. I remember her telling me she worked for 25 cents a day. One lady she worked for had her gathering up the fruit jars and washing them. Mom said I broke two of them, and she had to pay for them. Mom only owned two dresses at that time. She would wash the one while she wore the other. As I have said, times were unbelievably hard for many people in those days.

9
CALICO ROCK, ARKANSAS

The nearest city to Boswell was Calico Rock, above the bluffs on the beautiful White River. Calico had only one main street. The street ran east and west. It came to an end at the river bank after you crossed the railroad tracks. There was a ferry boat connected to a cable to keep it from being swept down the river with the current. If I remember correctly, there was room for about three cars or wagon teams on it.

Stores lined both sides of the street. The north side of the street was about ten feet higher than the buildings on the south side. From the street level, one had to climb steps up to all the stores on the north side. Whoever did the city planning, must have been drunk on Izard County moonshine.

The same layout existed on the back of the stores on the south side of the street. Few, if any customers entered any store from that side. It was about four stories below the street level. It was on that back side where the farmers parked their wagons, and secure their teams, providing some hay for them while the owners did shopping and visiting with old friends. Since we did not own a car at that time, we rode in an iron-wheeled wagon which was pulled by two horses, Maud and Dolly.

Calico had one movie theater. The building looked like it was left over from the Civil War. It was there I saw my first movie. It was in black and white. If my memory is correct, it was The Yearling, a story about a baby deer raised by a farm family and their young son. There were also a couple of cafes, where I had my first hamburger with fries. The burger and fries with a cola cost twenty-five cents. Today Calico Rock is a ghost town. In 2013, the population of the town was 1,521. Main Street is dead, and there is not one business establishment visible. Wikipedia offers additional details about this once thriving town.

http://en.wikipedia.org/wiki/Calico_Rock,_Arkansas.

10
WASHINGTON BOUND

Uncle Henry (Moody) Pierce was married to mom's second sister, Aunt Louise. They had a large family of eight children. There were two sets of twins. Earl and Burl, the oldest, then a sister Joan; followed by another set of twins names Earlene and Darlene. There were also young brothers. The family traveled to California and Washington to work in the cotton fields in Bakersfield, and the apple orchards in Wenatchee Valley. They returned to Boswell after the harvest. Since there was very little work in Izard County, mom decided that next spring the two of us would go to Washington and join the Pierces, where she would work in the orchards.

Mom bought tickets to Wenatchee, Washington, and we boarded the train for the twenty-one hundred mile ride. I had ridden the train once to Calico Rock, which was about eight miles north.

Between Boswell and Calico Rock, there was a small community, called Creswell. There was a sidetrack where the passenger train could pull off and let a freight train through. The train we were on pulled to the sidetrack. When I looked out the window, I saw about five young children sitting on flat rocks and watching the train. I remember waving to them, and they waved back. Little did I know that one of those little blond girls would become my wife.

The train ride was a new experience for me. I was about seven years old and was curious to find out everything I could about the train. The soap dispenser in the bathroom was most intriguing. I remember emptying it and putting every bit of the soap on my hair. I parted my hair in the middle and went out to show it off to mom. She did not think it was funny. Other than that, the ride was uneventful.

The Pierces met us at the train station and took us to their home in Monitor. It was about eight miles west of Wenatchee. The Pierces lived in an old army barracks located in the Shannon orchards next to the mountains west of Monitor. Apple and pear orchards covered the entire Wenatchee valley and mountains. Mom worked in the orchard.

I caught a school bus to school. Riding a bus was a new experience for me. However, concerning school, I have already let my thoughts be known. They had not changed, if anything, they were getting worse. I hated school. There was not anyone I knew, and I certainly did not know the subject material. That whole experience was a blur. Once, on the way to the bus stop, I purposely knelt down in a mud puddle so I would not have to go to school. I told my mother I fell in it. I do not know if she believed me or not, but I stayed home that day.

Next fall, after apple harvest, we returned to Boswell. While we were working in Washington, Grandpa Byler had purchased a large two-story house in Boswell. It had a gray exterior of plaster. It was across the lane, on the west side of the railroad tracks and next to White River. The back of the house extended over the bank of the river. Like the white house, some of my fondest memories center at their home. Mom and I lived with them again, but this time we were in Boswell.

The house set back from the railroad tracks about 75 feet. When the freight trains came through at night, they shook the beds. The track was partially in the front yard. We had plenty of time to play on those tracks. We would see who could walk furthest on a rail before falling off. When we heard the train coming, we would take a penny and lay it on the rail. After a mile long train had flattened the penny, old Abe was barely visible. The excitement of the train speeding through our little town was a great event to us. Occasionally we could give the engineer the signal, and he would blow the horn for us. Many summer evenings we ran up and down the tracks catching lightening bugs and putting them in a Mason fruit jar. Sometimes we would rub the bugs on ourselves, and we would glow in the dark for a while.

Across the tracks, and about two hundred feet north of Grandpa's house was the train depot. Just north of it were the water tank and a coal bin where the steam engine would add water and coal to keep the boiler going.

A ticket agent was on duty to sell tickets, and ship the freight to its proper destination. The train brought the mail, supplies for the two stores, and personal mail order items. Its arrival was a big event in Boswell. My first bicycle came from Sears to that old depot. Some of the people in our town shipped large cans of milk and cream. Others would load fence post they had cut by hand from cedar trees. Farmers would bring bales of hay or other items they might have to sell. These items were a source of income for them. When the engineer was ready to roll, he would blow the horn twice, let off a cloud of steam, and the big iron wheels would spin as he pushed the throttle forward. If you were near the depot, you could expect to be showered with black coal cinders.

Boswell had two stores that were about a hundred and fifty yards apart; no other buildings were between them. Thurman Smith owned the store closest to the tracks. It was the only store in Boswell for many years. It served as a post office and the general store where you could practically find anything you wanted. A farmer could buy feed for his animals. The carpenter could buy any size nail, and women bought beautiful cloth to make dresses and shirts. Even the flour sacks were imprinted cloth and used for shirts and blouses.

Later, another store, about a hundred and fifty yards east of the Smith store, was built. The road or "the lane" was between the two stores. The lane was of fine white sand. It was a great place to play games. The last time I was in Boswell, all the stores, and most houses were ghostly remnants of bygone days. Sadly, Boswell is a ghost town.

After school, some kids raced down the hill to the store. We would search to see if today's train had brought anything new. Since there was no electricity in town, ice cream was a special treat, if it was available. It would be in Dixie Cups with a wooden spoon provided. It was kept cold on dry ice. If Grandpa was at the store, I was in luck. I would ask for a nickel, and he never turned me down. I would set on the porch and dangle my feet over the edge while savoring every bite.

Although there was not a garage or gas station in Boswell, there was a gas pump across the road from the store. The gas pump was a tall round metal tank with a glass globe at the top. The globe was round and about three feet tall. It could hold ten gallons of gas. The tank had a handle by which you pumped the gas into the globe by hand. Markings were on the globe to let you know how much gas you were getting. The gas then flowed down to the waiting cars.

Several families from Izard County traveled to eastern Arkansas to pick strawberries. The only accommodations for workers were tents. There was a pump house nearby where some workers slept. I remember one of the families had a young daughter. Her name was Shirley Moody. Shirley was getting into her sleeping bag, and a scorpion had crawled in ahead of her. It stung her on the back. It must have been an awful painful ordeal because she cried for many hours.

When the work in the berry fields was over, some workers traveled to the northeast corner of Arkansas to pick cotton. This area, called "the bottoms" was lowland close to the Mississippi River. Flooding was common in that area. Many of the houses were built on piers or stilts to protect them from the floodwaters. The railroad tracks were on a leveey for the same reason. In places, you could see cotton fields on both sides of the tracks.

Mom and I stayed with the Pierce family while working the cotton fields. Mom took a pillowcase and sewed a strap that would fit over my shoulder. I had my cotton sack. I doubt that I filled the sack with cotton once during the whole season. I had an aversion to menial work. Also, the people in the "bottom land" considered "hill people" to be lazy. I didn't want to disappoint them.

I remember walking down the tracks to the store to buy candy with Earl, Burl, and Joan, my cousins. We had to cross on a trestle that was high above the still deep stagnate water below. Among the debris, a dead goat was floating on top of the water. No doubt, it drowned in the floodwaters.

For some reason unknown to me, mom and I returned to Boswell by ourselves. That experience stands out in my mind because we rode on a freight train. We were riding in the caboose. It was an exciting experience for a young boy. It was fall, and the other migrant workers would be making their return to the hill country in the Ozarks soon.

11
BACK TO WASHINGTON

Next spring we loaded into Uncle Moody's truck and headed for Washington again. This time, Grandpa and Grandma Byler, and my uncle Clarence came along. I think there was a total of eleven in the pickup truck. When we arrived we located on the Lower Monitor Road. We were about five miles west of Wenatchee and ten miles east of Cashmere. The road was blacktop and exited left off Highway 2, through the many orchards. It reconnected to Highway 2 after winding through the orchards for about five miles. The adults had found work at Moore's orchards. Noble Sanders owned an orchard just across the road. That was where Dwayne who became one of my best friends lived. We were glad to be back in Washington.

Mr. Moore provided small cabins for his workers. The cabins were located in the orchard just off the road. They were about ten by twelve feet in size. Mom and I lived in a cabin with two rooms. Grandpa and Grandma Byler lived in the other room. Uncle Clarence was single and had his private cabin. There were two other cabins. One was empty, and an old bachelor lived in the other. The Pierce family found work in another orchard in the Monitor area across the Wenatchee River. I was about age ten at the time.

One thing I will never forget was that Grandpa was mad at Grandma. I have no idea what the problem was. Mom said he was jealous for some reason. I am sure he had been drinking. The three of us, Grandma, my mother, and I were sitting on the bed. He was standing in front of us with a loaded pistol. I heard him say he was going to kill all three of us. My only response was to cry. Grandma continued talking to him until he walked out and left us alone. I never did learn for sure what that issue was. I am only thankful that Grandma was there, and was able to persuade him to change his mind.

12
BACK TO BOSWELL
AND THE SHOCK

That winter we were back in Boswell, and the one room school house again. The reader can understand by now that it was impossible for me to get an education under those circumstances.

Some of my best memories are of the time I spent in the little school house in Boswell. Not that I learned any academics, but it was there I made some friendships that have lasted a lifetime. Time and memory fail me to mention all who had some influence on me. Their faces, however, have not left my memory.

However, there was a more horrific shock than getting back to school. My mother informed me that she and the old bachelor, who lived in the cabin next door, would be getting married. Well, I can tell you, that news did not set well with me. My mother was mine, and I had no interest in sharing her with anyone. Three is a crowd. However, my feelings and protest did little good. The one room school didn't seem bad at all compared to this bad news.

After my mother and Earl Blue were married, we moved a few miles north of Boswell to where Uncle John owned several acres of property. He raised cattle, and chickens, and did some farming. Uncle John gave me a young white face calf. Later I sold it back to him and bought my first bicycle.

We lived in a small house on Uncle John's property located near Piney Creek. My stepdad tried his hand at farming, but he found it impossible to make enough money to live. It was difficult enough for those who owned the land. It was impossible for sharecroppers.

My step dad was a hard worker and did everything he could to provide. He was a good man and a good father to me. I regret that I was too young and selfish to see that until many years later. He plowed the bottom land owned by Uncle John. He plowed with two horses that pulled a turning plow. I remember seeing my dad follow those horses all day long. The furrow was straight and deep. I asked him to let me try. I think I had plowed up three rows before he got it under control. I ask how he was able to keep the furrow so straight. He pointed to a white flag on a post at the other end of the field. He said he keep that flag in view between the two horses.

The house provided by Uncle John was a simple, two room building. My guess is, it was about twenty feet wide, and thirty feet long. The kitchen, the bed, and the wood stove were all in that one room. The outside consisted of rough one by eight planks. Strips of one by two's nailed over the cracks between the boards kept the wind and rain out. It was unpainted, and there was no official foundation under it. The foundation consisted of flat rocks stacked at each corner and midpoints. That was the foundation of many similar homes. Nor was the house anchored to the ground. I am amazed to this day that a blast of wind didn't send it sailing through the air into Piney Creek.

My mother and stepdad nailed cardboard to the inside walls. Mom ordered wallpaper from a Sears catalog. It had a beautifully printed pattern. She mixed flour and water to make paste or glue. The paste was applied to the backside of the wallpaper, and the paper applied to the cardboard. The finishing touch was a trim that came with the wallpaper and applied to the top of the project, near the ceiling. Mom was proud that she had improved the appearance of our house.

It was a wonderful time of my life, living next to Uncle John Byler. That meant that I had constant playmates in Jimmy Dale and Jonny Wayne. In the summer, we spent lots of time playing and swimming in Piney Creek. Piney Creek was flanked on the north side with sheer rock cliffs of well over one hundred feet high. On the side near our house was a natural sand bar. Large trees grew along the creek bank. These had grape vines growing in them. Jim and I would swing on the vines and plunge into the water. Piney was where I learned to swim, and it was there I also got one of the worst sunburns in my life. Large blisters, filled with liquid were all over my back. I believe my mother made a paste of vinegar and soda powder and dabbed it on the blisters. That brought some relief.

Jimmy Dale and I owned bee bee guns. Mine was a Red Rider model. Mom fixed a sack lunch for us, and we went into the woods looking for lizards, snakes, frogs, and any other wild game we could find. After about thirty minutes of hunting, it was time to eat. Therefore, we sat on a flat rock or a log and ate our sandwiches. We also created a reptile cemetery where we buried our bounty. We used pieces of colored glass as tombstones. Those were great days for two young boys.

The one room school house in Boswell was located high on a tableland hill that overlooked Boswell and the beautiful White River Valley. Mom fixed a lunch which she packed in my Lone Ranger dinner pail. She walked part way with me to school. When we came to the path that cut across the holler and up the hill to the school, she kissed me, and I would go on my way to school.

Although education was not important to our family, some of my best memories are of the time I attended the school house in Boswell. I learned very little when it came to academics. There wasn't any help or encouragement from home. In fact, our home was wherever mom could find work. The constant moving from house to house, town to town, and state to state caused me to lose all interest in studies. Thus, I failed to learn the basics in reading, writing, and arithmetic. The lack of these left me with much insecurity that has always plagued me.

My only interest was the social part of the school. Eldon Neel was a lifelong friend to me. In addition, every young man sees a girl he likes. Thus, Wilma Jean Qualls was that girl. I think she knew it and also liked me. I was about eleven years old at the time. However, mom and I left Boswell again, and Jean and Eldon married years later. They moved to Mountain Home and lived there until Eldon's death November 23, 2009. They were married for fifty-one years and seven months when Eldon died from a heart attack.

I thank God that I had the opportunity to visit with them before his death. Eldon loved the Lord, and it will be great to see him again.

To this day, my mind keeps going back to that school house on the hill.

Eldon had a beautiful black quarter horse named Smokey. You would see him riding it around town and to school. I don't remember ever seeing Smokey with a bridle or saddle. Eldon would guide him by applying pressure to Smokey's sides with his legs. Smokey bonded to Eldon like a little puppy.

Eldon was the one friend that seemed like a brother to me. He, his parents, and one sister, Nadine, lived on the left side of the dirt road that came into Boswell from the north. It was the first house on the edge of town. I spent many days and nights in that little house with him and his family. Eldon had the kind of personality that would attract anyone. I can't imagine anyone disliking him. The Qualls home was located just above the Neel's

I thank God for the impact for my teacher's example. Miss Erma McNeal was a devout Christian, and read the Bible and prayed at the beginning of each school day. I am confident that she played a great part in my salvation and ministry. Although I don't remember the lessons she taught, I learned to respect her unwavering example. The Bible reading by Grandpa, the songs and stories by my mother, and the ministry of Miss Erma created in me a deep faith in God.

It was necessary to walk to the spring to get drinking water for the students. I remember on one occasion the teacher allowed my cousin Johnny Wayne and me to go for water. The spring was at the bottom of a hill, and so we decided we would kick the bucket ahead of us. I can't remember if it held water or not. Neither do I remember if our story held water, probably not.

The only reason I looked forward to school was to see my friends and play the games. We played tag, dare base, and anti-over, and any others we could invent.

Not all the experiences were positive. I spent much of my time at school standing with my nose in a corner. That was one form of discipline for disobedience. I'm thankful I didn't get caught each time I disobeyed, or I would not have a nose left.

There were two doors to the front porch of the schoolhouse. A sign made of six by six-inch cardboard hung on a string by each door. One was for the girls, and the other was for the boys; they were so marked, and on one sign were written "in," and on the other "out." When you left, you were to turn the sign to the out position. When you returned, you were to turn it to the in position.

On one occasion I spent too much time at the outhouse. The teacher came to get me, and with a switch encouraged me to hurry back to class. I think a special note should be added here. There was no outhouse for the boys. Like we had at the white house, it was down a bank, and out of sight of the school. The girls did have an outhouse. That was before we had heard of equal rights.

I believe the school grades were 1-7. Those in the upper grades had to go about five miles to Piney Creek. A swinging footbridge built across the creek consisted of four steel cables extended across the creek. They were parallel to each other. Two other cables were about four feet above the other two. Boards were attached to the lower cables. Smaller cables were attached *vertically* from the lower cables to the upper ones. These were attached in such a way to provide stability and protection on the sides of the bridge. There was a reason it was called a "swinging bridge."

The bus from Calico Rock would pick up the students. I remember walking that bridge many times. Today, a nice traffic bridge connecting the roads crosses the creek.

13
BACK TO WASHINGTON - AGAIN

My mother and stepdad decided it was hopeless to continue farming in Arkansas. Therefore, they packed up dads 39 Desoto, and we were off to Washington again. We returned to where my mother and Earl first met. Mr. Moore gave dad a job. The Sanders family also had an orchard just across the road, and Mr. Sanders provided us a place to live in his apple shed. He also gave dad part time work.

Our living quarters consisted of two rooms portioned off within a shed for freshly picked apples awaiting shipping to a Wenatchee cold storage. The shed had a sink and a cold water spigot. The toilet was an outhouse. Mom nailed wooden apple boxes on the walls for a place to put the glasses, plates, and cooking pans. These were her cupboards. We also used apple boxes for chairs. The shed provided all the comforts we needed. Mr. Sanders had three boys. Dwayne was two years older than me. We became best of friends and spent many days together.

We were living on the Lower Monitor Road, about five miles west of Wenatchee near highway two, also called Easy Street. Apple orchards lined both sides of the road. Dad was offered jobs by two other farmers in the general area. Once again I was shuttled off from one school to another.

One of the advantages of living on the lower Monitor Road was a pretty little blond girl by the name of Linda DeShazo. She lived nearby. I had a bicycle with a carriage rack on the back where Linda would sit. Of course, she had to put her arms around me for safety. I was thankful I was there for her safety.

There was also a natural swimming hole nearby. Backwater from the Wenatchee River and a small stream created a perfect place to swin. All the kids in the community gathered there to swim and play. It was there I first discovered why I liked Linda. I didn't have sisters, so she was a novelty to me. Don't read in that more than you should. We simply were very good friends. However, a pretty girl in a swimming suit is more educational than any biological textbook. At this writing, Linda and I are still friends on Facebook, a social network. She was, and still is a wonderful person.

In addition, it was at that swimming hole I almost lost one of my best friends. Jack Wright and I were swimming, and Jack was caught in an undercurrent and swept out into the Wenatchee River. He kept trying to swim upstream against the current, but to no avail. He went under and disappeared. That was my second religious experience. I remember falling to my knees and praying for God to save Jack. Although I was not a Christian, I did believe in God and that He could answer prayer. To my amazement, Jack was washed out on the river bank about a hundred feet below the old swimming hole. He had swallowed about half of the Wenatchee River, but in a few minutes, he was as good as new.

14
THE SHOCKING TRUTH
MADE KNOWN

I walked about a quarter of a mile to the bus stop where the Lower Monitor Road connected to Highway two. While waiting for the bus, Carol DeShazo, Linda's older sister, said to me, "I know something about you that you don't know." She refused to tell me.

After school, I told my mother about the comment. I am sure my mother had dreaded that this day would come. She had told me in the past that my biological father was dead. She did not have a picture of him, and I knew absolutely nothing about his present location. Neither did I know that she was never married to him. She told me his name, where she met him and where he had lived, that's all. Needless to say, I was upset with my mother for about a week, but I had a good stepfather, and it was soon forgotten. You don't miss what you never had.

This may be the best place to explain facts about my biological father, whom I had never met. It was while mom was working the cotton fields in 1937, she met a man named Cheston Davis. I don't know any of the details, but she told me he was very handsome, with black wavy hair. She said I looked just like him. It was there and at that time I was conceived. As I mentioned elsewhere, you never miss what you never have. However, around 2009 I became curious and tried to locate him on the internet. I was not successful, but I have a cousin who is a detective in Wenatchee, Washington. With the little information I had, she was able to locate where he was buried.

I called the funeral home and explained to the contact who I was, and who I was searching for. He said he remembered the funeral and that Cheston Davis Junior lived in town. He located his phone number and I made the call. It took some explaining, but in time, with the details I had, he was sure my story was accurate.

Joyce and I had planned to go to Arkansas. Cheston and I made plans to meet. We met in Walnut Ridge, Arkansas at the Catfish House. We had a wonderful lunch and spent some time together. I felt instant love for Cheston Junior, his wife, and Sisters, Millie and Peggy Sue. There are other members of the family, but it was not possible to meet with them. My one regret is that I did not know of these events much sooner, our family could have spent more years together.

Next spring, dad took a job in another orchard along Highway 2, about five miles east of Monitor. Living quarters was another Apple shed. I was about fourteen at that time. We were in that shed about a year or so. Next spring dad found a job as orchard boss about two miles east of where we were. The house was beautiful. It was on the North side of Easy Street. It overlooked a beautiful valley that contained hundreds of orchards and a view of the beautiful Wenatchee River. The house had a beautiful lawn and a huge oak tree in the middle of the yard, which they kept manicured. Mom and dad stayed put in that house for many years.

That fall, I enrolled in Junior High School at Sunny- slope. I spent three years there and had plenty of time to meet and make new friends. Three years was the longest I had spent in any of the dozen schools I attended. The one room school in Boswell was one, and the other was at Sunnyslope. I have many fond memories of these two. It was a time I made friends for a lifetime. Some were Dwayne Sanders, Dennis and Bobby Britt, Jr. and John Fortune, Jack Wright, Carol Jones, and Margo Zude. I spent most of those years with these friends.

Dennis and I became the best of friends. We spent much time in each other's home. He lived on Birch Mountain. Crestview road led up the hill through apple orchards to his house. It was about a mile and a half from the school. It was about the same distance from where he headed up the hill, to my house.

Dennis' family was musically inclined, and my love for country music made the bond that much stronger. He would come to my house, and we pretend we were singing at the Grand Old Opera. The light switch string that hung from the ceiling provided us a make-believe microphone. The mop and the broom were our make-believe musical instruments. After mom and dad had gone to bed, Dennis and I spent hours entertaining ourselves with our make-believe talent.

Dad had a fancy cigarette stand that had an electric lighter and a storage cup for cigarettes. Dennis and I would take two cigarettes, and go to the outhouse and smoke them. In a matter of time we were hooked, and loved the taste of cigarettes. It was about seven to eight years before I gave up the habit. I have no idea if Dad ever knew that he was contributing to our new vice.

In time, Dennis and I each purchased guitars and set about to learn to play them. I bought a beautiful flat top E. C. Martin guitar. I paid a little more than $100.00 for it. Now it sells for $3400.00. We spent every free hour, either at my house or his, trying to learn some new chords. Finally, we learned G, C, and D chords and managed to play a few songs together. Dennis learned to play lead guitar and was very good. His style was like Chet Atkins. Me, I never got beyond a few chords. However, my friendship with the Britt family deepened as we spent those wonderful days together. It was in the orchard I met Jerry Britt, Dennis' older brother. He and I became friends quickly. He loaned me his guitar, and we also traded comic books. One morning I went to his small home to trade books with him. His wife came to the door and informed me that Jerry had drowned in Three Lakes the night before. That was a devastating time for all of us.

Mom and dad also worked on Birch Mountain thinning apples. The weather was hot. I secured a burlap bag because I had a plan to make some money. I bought cold bottled soft drinks and a variety of candy bars and sold them to the workers. They were glad to get the refreshments, and I was glad to take their money.

15
RUNAWAY TO CALIFORNIA

Dennis and I got a job working at the local movie theater. The city allowed the theater to place frames in various locations. The frames were made of aluminum, and had glass locking doors. The poster inserts were in full color and promoted the upcoming movies. Our pay was fifty-five cents per hour. The task took about two hours. Once we were paid, we went to the corner soda store. We bought a pack of cigarettes, soda, and put the rest in the pinball machines.

We also worked nights at the Mountain View drive in theater. It was our job to use flashlights and signal where cars were to park. We also handed the speaker to the customer and assisted him to hang it on the inside of the window.

Many nights we would work to one in the morning and then walk along Highway 2 to our homes. After Dennis turned on to the street to his house, I was alone on the dark highway. Needless to say, I was scared much of the time. A pocket full of rocks gave me some comfort.

Dennis and I were at his house playing music and smoking our cigarettes one afternoon. The kids were in school, and the adults were working in the orchards. We were bored and needed wheels to go to town. Dennis' dad came home for some reason, and Dennis asked if he could use the car. That request was turned down, it turned into an argument, and if my memory is correct, Dennis received a slap on the face. That ended the music and the boredom.

Dennis was mad and decided to take the car after his dad went back to work. We attempted to start the car, but it would not start. Dennis looked under the hood and saw that the coil wire was disconnected. He had the problem fixed in minutes, and we were making plans.

Our plans included a trip to California. We went to my house, and I left a note for my mother. I grabbed a large can of grapefruit juice and $21.00 that I had in my room. So, with $21.00, my guitar, and a can of grapefruit juice, we were on our way to California.

I didn't know a soul in California, nor had I ever been there. Dennis had an Uncle in Stockton, so that became our destination. When we arrived, the forty-one Ford had serious problems. Dennis and his Uncle pulled the heads and discovered a crack in the block. That was serious. We were in California with a broken car and no money. I contacted my mother for a bus ticket back to Wenatchee. I left Dennis with his Uncle and his problem. To this day, I have no idea how that event ended.

I'm sure things were not good between him and his dad after that. He never said anything to me about it, but he later told me he was going to join the Air Force. I have not seen Dennis since he joined. That was around 1954. However, I located him through one of his family members, and we made contact by email in 2010.

According to Dennis' daughters, he was making plans to come to Washington to visit me. Sadly, a brain aneurysm took his life October 25, 2015. Thankfully, one of his daughters, Kelly, and I are friends on Facebook.

16
THE SUNNYSLOPE SCHOOL

There were many things about the Sunnyslope School I enjoyed. One was the cute little girl by the name of Margo. I have no idea how we met. I was about fourteen, and she was my first real girlfriend. I thought I was in love, and I believed she felt the same. I spent many hours at her house. Her mother and father were very accepting of me. Margo had three younger sisters. They were Lana, Darlene, and Charlene who were twins.

Margo was a grade ahead of me, and after her transfer to Wenatchee High school, we lost contact with each other. Our departure was as mysterious as our meeting. She met a young man, and in time they were married. Our meeting and our departure were alike, a fog to me, and all details escape my mind. I was very young and naive. If any good came of our relationship, it was at her house Dennis Britt met Carol Jones.

Dennis had met the girl that would become his wife at Margo's house. Carol Jones lived across School Street from Margo. Margo and Carol lived about a hundred yards south of the Sunnyslope Church. In time, I lost contact with the three of them. It was some years before I knew that Carol and Dennis had married. Dennis also informed me it was on the same day the twin towers were destroyed that Carol had died of a heart attack.

My friend, Dwayne Sanders, could pass for 21. He owned a 1952 Mercury, and an old army jeep. When Dwayne got behind the wheel, you would have thought you were in the Bat-o-mobile. Not only did Dwayne have the car; a car meant, girls, and he was able to buy beer and wine for us. My first drink was White Port that Dwayne purchased.

One Saturday night, Dwayne, Dennis, and I were cruising the streets of Wenatchee. We decided we need something to drink. A tavern was on the southern outskirts of town. Dwayne parked and went inside and purchased a twenty-four bottle case of Olympia Beer. Just as he was putting it in the trunk, a police car drove by. He made a quick U-turn and pulled behind the car. He could tell by looking at Dennis and me that we were not twenty-one, the age required to buy alcohol. He asked to see Dwayne's license and gave it back to him. Then he said," let me see that license again." When he realized that Dwayne was only eighteen, he wanted to know who sold the beer to him. Dwayne told him it was the bartender. The officer went inside, and of course, the bartender denied selling it to him. By this time a man came out and was observing from the porch. Since the bartender had lied, I told the man on the porch that the bartender had better be out of town by midnight. The man on the porch when directly to the officer, and told him of my threat. The officer came, opened the car doors and placed us in his car. He took us to the police station. He said something to me I will never forget. "You know, if something happened to that bartender, you would be in very deep trouble because of your comment." I understood and agreed. I believe Dwayne was fined thirty-five dollars. He also had to call someone to take us back to his car.

Both Dennis and Dwayne had their driver's license. I would ask Dad if we could borrow his car if one of the others drove. It was a 1947 four doors black Chevrolet. I don't remember him turning us down. However, as soon as we were out of sight of the house, the designated driver pulled over, and I slid under the wheel. I was driving all over Wenatchee and age fourteen without a license.

We borrowed the car again to go rabbit hunting south of Wenatchee, near the city of Quincy. Sagebrush was thick, and rabbits were abundant. I think there were four of us in the car. We drove along a dirt road, and when we saw a rabbit, we loaded our 22 and shot from the window. It became too burdensome to reload and unload each time we saw a rabbit, so we left the guns loaded. I saw a rabbit, grabbed my gun to shoot, but the shell did not fire. I had no memory of firing that bullet and failing to eject it. I later discovered that the gun had fired in the car and shot a hole in the roof of Dad's Chevrolet. I took two rocks and flattened out the hole as best I could. I never told him about it. I think he may have discovered in months later. I doubt that he ever loaned us his car again.

I had missed all hopes of an educational foundation, the academics at Sunnyslope were almost impossible for me. I did manage to make it through the eighth grade and was ready for the new school in Wenatchee next year. I may have attended a month or so, but soon discovered that I was in over my head. That fall found me sitting in a 9th-grade classroom in Wenatchee. I might as well be sitting on the moon. Nothing in the Algebra textbook made sense. It might as well been Swahili. If I was way in over my head at Sunnyslope, I was at the bottom of the ocean in Wenatchee. So why try? I have no idea how many days I attended, but it couldn't have been many.

Two other friends and I skipped for a few days. When I returned, I discovered I had been expelled from school. I also learned how to be accepted by my peers, which led to more smoking, drinking, playing music, and looking for girls.

As I look back, I'm glad none of my friends were wicked, compared to today's standards. In fact, as I reflect, I believe Dwayne Sanders was a Christian. I know he did a few things that one shouldn't do. However, I don't remember ever hearing him using a curse word, or being vile. We were four good ole' boys searching for fun. None were disrespectable or destructive to property. I am well aware that most of us were unsaved. Some nights we would park in the churchyard at Sunnyslope and entertain ourselves by listen to western music from Del Rio, Texas, and drinking Olympia Beer. I don't want to gloss over my life. I was wicked enough to deserve the fires of hell. However, I'm too ashamed to discuss my sinful life, and it would not edify or improve on the story of my journey.

Almost every Saturday night, in the summer, one of the local Grange halls in the valley would have dancing featured by country music. Since all of us were addicted to country music and pretty girls, the Grange became our Saturday night destination. It was a place you could act like a fool, and not be out of place or noticed.

One Saturday night John Fortune and I went dancing in the small town of Peshastin. The Dude Smith family provided the music. It was there I first heard Bonnie Guitar sing her hit song, Dark Moon. The Smiths had two beautiful daughters who were singing that night. John and I walked down to get a better look. The girls smiled at us, and we were in love.

We found out that they would be in the city of Snohomish the following Saturday night. Therefore, we drove from Wenatchee to Snohomish, to see the girls, we were sure they would be thrilled to see us. What a wake-up call! When we got there, they wouldn't even glance at us. We were crushed. Truly, love hurts.

On another occasion, Dwayne, Jr, Dennis, and I went dancing at one of the Grange Halls in Peshastin. Jr. had too much to drink and was getting sick. I reach forward and hit the automatic window button to allow him some fresh air. After a few minutes, I rolled the window up because of the cold. It was in the dead of winter. Jr. jerked and tried to move his head. He said, "Boys, boys, something's got a hold of me!" I checked to see. I had rolled the window up on his hair. That event was worth the evening.

17
THE GIRL OF MY LIFE

Two friends, I always envied were Jr. and John Fortune. It seemed that everything about them was perfect. They dressed to the max, and Jr. had a 1948 Buick convertible that was to die to own. It always shined like a diamond, and he always had a pretty girl with him. I guess that's the secret. Guys are looking for pretty girls, and girls are looking for pretty cars.

One night at the Fish Net, a fish and fries drive-in, I saw Jr. Fortune in his big shiny Buick convertible with the prettiest girl I had ever seen. Life was unfair. Just because he had the coolest car in town, did not give him the right to have the prettiest girl in town. I was breathless. I called him the next day and said, "Hey, old friend, I simply must go out with her." He said, "She won't date you." I said, "You want to bet?" He said, "Yes."

Some days later, he drove me to her house at Birch Mountain. She lived about half a mile from the Britt family on Birch Mountain. I explained the bet I had with Jr. and ask her if she would be willing to go on a date with me. Her response was "Yes." The moral is, don't ever trust your best friend around your girlfriend.

I had lied about my age and was able to get my driver's license, and the girl. I was fifteen. Dad loaned me his car, and I was at Joyce's house ahead of time. Our date would be a surprise. I was sure she would like it. What a surprise I had coming!

When she came to the door, she was a vision to behold. She had a skirt with a full crinoline. Those were trendy in the fifties, and they made the skirt bell-shaped when it stood out at the hem of the garment. No doubt, they were intended to make the waist appearance smaller. A sweater, a scarf around her neck, and a smile that would make the moon blush. I felt like a king. Here I was, fifteen years old, a pack of cigarettes in my pocket, my dad's four door Chevrolet, and the prettiest girl in the state seated beside me. I was the man, and Jr. was the loser. I felt so sad for him... know what I mean?

When we arrived at the scene of the party, a bonfire was already going on the beach down near the Columbia River. Joyce asked, "What is this?" I told her it was a beach party. She said, "Well, you will need to take me home so I can put on some suitable clothes. What I am wearing will never do." I took her home, she made a quick change, and we were back at the beach.

I confess that I have no memory of the events at the party. I was not drinking, but my mind is blank on that subject. However, on the way home, things were different. I pulled the old Chevy into the church parking lot upon Sunnyslope, where I had parked before with my buddies and drank beer and listened to western music, I am sure Joyce and I found things to talk about, but again I don't remember what they were. There was one thing I do remember that I said. I told her, "I am going to marry you." I can't imagine that she said anything other than "yes." She later assured me she thought I was crazy. I admit it; I was, and I still am.

On another occasion, I went to her house to pick her up. Someone noticed me pull into the driveway and came out to greet me. I informed them that I would wait in the car until Joyce was ready to go. Her father sent someone out to inform me that I would *not* wait in the car; I would be coming in. I went in. They were just sitting down for supper, and her father insisted that I join them. I did. I still remember the mouthwatering biscuits that Joyce had made. She is still the best cook I know, and all of us have waistlines to prove it.

Our dating was like the Seattle weather; each week it would change. One week it would be hotter than Death Valley in August. The next week it was as cold at Mount Everest. I am sure the cause of this was our immaturity. Both of us dated others a few times, but it seemed that we always found ourselves back together.

On one of our dates, the timing seemed just right to ask, "Will you marry me?" By now she was crazy about me and answered "yes." We visited jewelry stores searching for a ring that I could afford. I bought her an engagement ring. You needed the Hubble Telescope to see the diamond, but the salesman assured me one was there. Joyce loved it, I could afford it, and the salesman was happy. What a coincidence when you find three people who are all happy over the same thing, and at the same time.

Jr. Fortune, who introduced me to Joyce, was never thanked by me. However, as I look back, I think he was trying to get even with me. He gave me a call and asked if I would like to go to a movie with him. He still had the big blue Buick, and there was nothing I would like better than to ride in it with the top down. When he showed up, he had his new girlfriend in the front seat, and her younger sister in the back, where I was asked to sit. Again, most of the evening was a blur. I knew this was not a good setup - or was it? Did Junior set me up by seating me in the back seat with his girlfriend's sister?

After the movie, we drove to the local Fish Net hangout where most of the Wenatchee teens met. We pulled up to the window and ordered, and then found a parking spot. Who else do you think was in the parking lot? You guessed it. It was Joyce and two of her girlfriends. When I saw her, and she saw me, I knew I was dead. What excuse could I give that anyone would believe? As she started walking toward the car, I knew she was a woman on a mission. The only thing I remember was the engagement ring flying at me. I picked it up and put it in my pocket. When I looked up, she was nowhere near so I could explain. Even if she had been, what would I say that she would believe? That was our first and only divorce, so far.

Later that year, Dwayne Sanders and I heard there was work in Yakima in the Hop Fields. Dennis, Dwayne, Joyce, and I drove to Yakima to see about a job. They were desperate to get anyone they could, so Dwayne and I accepted the job. The living conditions were unbelievable. It was a twelve by twelve shack, made with planks with knotholes and cracks so wide you could count the stars. The cabin had two WWII bunks. That was all! The small wood stove was outside. That was where you cooked if you wanted a hot meal.

I drove the tractor that pulled the portable hop machine. The design of a hop field is difficult to describe. A series of wires secured to upright poles form a network, to which strings are secured, and extend down to the hop plant. The plant is a climbing vine which grows to the above network about ten feet from the ground. Hops are a bright green and resemble a small pine cone. They are one ingredient in beer. That may explain why some people who drink get hop-ing mad.

Dwayne and I were able to make it through the harvest, and then we had had enough of the hop fields. It was back to Wenatchee for us.

One enjoyable part of working in Yakima was that my cousins, Jimmy Dale and Johnny Wayne were there with their parents. It was good to be with them.

18
BACK TO ARKANSAS

I made another trip to Arkansas some months later. I spent most of my time with my friend, Eldon Neel. At that time he was dating Wilma Jean Qualls. They later married and were together for fifty-one years and seven months. Eldon died of a heart attack.

While in Arkansas, I met a young girl by the name of Marie Long. She, Eldon, Jean, and I went on a date together. Again, I have a very little memory of those events. She gave me several of her graduation pictures, which I treasured. I tried a few times to call her after returned to Washington, but she would not receive my calls. I can take a hint.

It was during this time that Joyce's dad had a heart attack and died. Sadly, I was not part of her life at that time and was not a comfort to any of the family. Her mother worked full time at night. Joyce and three sons were on their own.

The family moved to Wenatchee where Joyce found a job to help her mother with the bills. She worked, went to school, and did the housework for the family. There was no leadership or discipline in the family. Therefore, all the boys quit school. Joyce's mother tried marriage again, but it soon ended in divorce.

After returning to Washington from Arkansas, Joyce and I managed to get back on speaking terms. I have no idea what the process of events that led us back together again. This time, both of us were more serious about each other. I was at her house every free minute. Nothing could keep us apart. We were in love!

19
MY SALVATION

It was during those days that my mother invited me to go to church with her on Easter Sunday. I ask Joyce if she was willing to go. She said she would. We visited the First Baptist Church. The church was across the street from the Greyhound Depot on First Street and North Chelan Ave. The church has now moved to a more suitable location.

I don't remember a word of the sermon. However, at the end of the message, the pastor said, "If you aren't sure you're saved and going to heaven, you need to come and let someone show you how you can know." I had always believed in God and the Bible. However, I didn't know you could know for sure about heaven. I went forward, and a man took a Bible showing me that if I would ask the Lord to save me, He would. I asked Him, and He did! That was the beginning of a new life for me.

Joyce was in the twelfth grade and only a few months from graduation. However, I was persistent, and she dropped out of school to marry me. She has never let me forget that I kept her from graduating. I never let her forget what a wise decision she made.

I was barely seventeen, and Joyce was eighteen. We decided to go to Coeur d'Alene, Idaho to get married. The date was November 5th. 1955. Jim Collie, a special friend of mine, and his girlfriend, Dorothy

Arms joined us as witnesses. At this writing, Jim and Dorothy continue to be our friends and live in Wenatchee.

Jim's dad worked for Washington State and helped me secure a job with the state. I was assigned to the survey crew. It was a great job and paid a good salary. However, for some reason I quit. I have no idea why.

Jim's dad was working on Stevens Pass and the mirror on a truck hit him and killed him. Jim asked me to preach the funeral. It was my first, and I have no idea how I did. Nevertheless, The Collie family drove from Wenatchee and was in church that Sunday morning. That day, Jim accepted the Lord as his Savior.

We returned to Wenatchee and rented a small apartment on Mission Street. It was the same street where she had lived with her mother and three brothers. It was about a quarter mile south of where she had lived before. Their address was 316 South Mission Street. I love 3:16's.

I worked in cold storage in Cashmere, WA. It was about ten or twelve miles north of Wenatchee. It was a good job and paid $1.25 an hour. It was inside, and my job was to unload trucks and trailers as the apple farmers brought them in. We had hand trucks that would carry six boxes at a time. The boxes were taken to a designated place, and then I lifted two or three more boxes by hand and stacked them on top of the other six. They were in cold storage until the buyer came for them. Then they were taken to a packing shed and prepared for shipping.

Joyce and I lived in the apartment for about three months. The father of my friend, Dwayne Sanders, owned an orchard up in a canyon north of Dryden. I don't know who made the arrangements. No doubt it was my stepdad. Mr. Sanders offered to let us live in one of the houses on the property, rent free! We moved in January to a nice two bedroom house. It was eight miles north of where I worked in Cashmere.

That winter, 1955, we had at least five feet of snow. Buildings and sheds were collapsing because of the weight of the snow and ice. I was hired by some shed owners to shovel snow off the roofs of their buildings.

Most of the crew was laid off at the cold storage since the apple harvest was over. It was necessary to find a job working in the orchards. Winter was the time for pruning trees and picking up the props. The props were used in the summer as the apples matured. Without the props, the weight of the apples would break the limbs. After picking up the props, they were stacked together and leaned upright next to the trunk of the trees, ready for next year's harvest. These were cold and miserable jobs I disliked, but at least it was a job.

One day when I came home from work and Joyce was outside with a small fire burning. I notice she was deliberately and carefully placing one piece of paper at a time in the fire. I went over to inspect what was cooking. I discovered it was the graduation pictures that Marie Long had given to me on my last visit to Arkansas. I had overlooked them, so the memories of Marie went up in smoke.

Next spring Joyce was pregnant with our first son, Rocky. Many ask "why the name, Rocky?" That winter I worked for a farmer who lived a few miles further up the canyon from our house. I was pruning apple trees and picking up props. He had a son who worked with me, and his name was Rocky. I had never thought of that name, and it sounded good. So, Rocky, it was.

20
THE MOVE TO SEATTLE

The next summer, I went to Seattle and applied for a job at the Boeing Aircraft Company. A few days later, they contacted me and informed me they had a job for me. Joyce and I found a small house on Alki Point, in West Seattle.

I was hired by Boeing to install rivets. The job location was in Renton. It was about a forty minute drive to work across the Spokane viaduct, over the hill to Rainer Ave, and to the Boeing plant.

Riveting was not a difficult job unless you worked in the wing section or the forty-one section. That is where I started. The forty-one section included everything forward of the cabin bulkhead. In the first year, I was promoted to a grade five, which was thes highest pay grade you could go in that field.

It was while we lived in West Seattle, our first son Rocky was born. Joyce had been to a doctor in Cashmere, before our move to Seattle, and she wanted to continue with him. That meant each checkup amounted to a trip to eastern Washington. We did not have family or friends in Seattle, so we went back to Wenatchee every weekend. Rocky was born in December. Joyce had been staying with her sister the lasts six week of her pregnancy. It was a good thing she was close to the doctor when the time came. Rocky was a breach birth and had she not been in the hospital, both she and the baby would have died.

We were both excited over our newborn son! He was like a new toy with which to play. Joyce was in her best element as a parent. I have never seen anyone who was as serious about meeting every need of her children. They were never neglected one minute at anytime, by her.

I could not wait, so I drove to Cashmere and found a top of the line rocking horse. It was the real deal. It had all the features of a real horse; it was beautifully painted and held in place by four strong springs. It had a saddle and bridle reins built into it. I had Rocky on it before he could sit up or hold up his head. Together, we had fun learning. In time, he was riding it like a real cowboy. Those were some of our best years.

21
BACK TO WENATCHEE

After about four years at Boeing, I became dissatisfied. I quit my job; we packed up and moved back to Wenatchee. We lived with my parents until I found a job in the community of Rock Island, about eight miles south of Wenatchee. It was a smelting factory called Keokuk. Pig iron was made as an additive to harden aluminum.

I must have worked there for a year or so before I injured my back. I was using a shovel like a tool that looked somewhat like a pitchfork. I would get a shovel load and pitch it into a front end loader attached to a tractor. As I was shoveling, I twisted my back. It brought me to my knees. I was taken to the hospital in Wenatchee. That injury has plagued me all my life, and as I type these pages, I am still in constant pain. Needless to say, that ended that job.

It was back to the orchards and cold storage jobs. That was the only skills I had. The cold storage in Cashmere, where I had previously worked, hired me, and I was doing the same type of work as before.

22

BACK TO BOEING AND
THE TRANSFER TO MOSES LAKE

I returned to Seattle to see if Boeing would hire be again. Joyce was pregnant with Randy at this time. He too was born in Wenatchee. Within a few months, I transferred to Moses Lake, Washington at Larson Airbase to work on a modification program on the KC135. Several B-52 bombers were stationed there in a state of readiness. Boeing was using the base hangers to convert KC-135 tankers into Awax planes. A large, disc shaped radar dome was on top of the plane. The plane contained every kind of surveillance equipment, and served as the eye in the sky.

That move would change our lives forever. We located in the small town of Soap Lake. It was about twenty-five miles north of Moses Lake. I was working the night shift, and Joyce decided to attend a midweek service at the Baptist Church. She persuaded me to go the following Sunday. It was the first time we had been in church for several years.

The congregation was small, but they made up for it with their friendliness and reception of us. I liked the pastor. His name was David Douglass. He had attended College in New York and was an excellent Bible teacher. He must have felt out of place pastoring in a small farming town. He had a wonderful wife and two small girls. Pastor Douglass made that small church a great place for us.

At that time, Joyce and I had two small boys, Rocky and Randy. By God's grace, there was a young family in the church who also had two young boys. This couple had been in the church all their life. Their names are Leroy and Florence Friend. Leroy was a deacon, a Sunday school teacher, and Superintendent in the Church. Their two boys and ours became instant friends and are to this day.

Leroy came up to me after church, and after some small talk, asked if we would be available to come to their house after the evening service and have apple pie and ice cream. I told them we would. Not only was that Sunday, our first time in church in years, but we also loved it so much we committed to another service next Sunday!

Over the months, we became the best of friends with Leroy and Florence Friend. We were together every week, and Leroy was guiding me in the Scriptures to a point where the Bible became the central part of our life. The Pastor started a Bible class in the attic of the church. Each Monday night, four of us men, along with the Pastor, would study Bible doctrine together. I was being grounded in God's Word and loved every class.

Many old sinful habits were still in my life. The strongest addiction I had was cigarettes and profanity. I can honestly say that I loved the cigarettes. Although Leroy never said a word about my smoking, something was happening in my life. The more I read and heard the Bible, the more guilt I felt about this habit. I knew I needed to quit.

Even God must have laughed at my pretend prayers and puny attempts to kick the habit. I would say a prayer, smoke a pipe or cigar, or roll my own in an attempt to quit gradually. But nothing worked. However, in time I became desperate, and my prayers became sincere.

One evening at work, I was talking to a coworker about my desire to quit smoking. He asked why I wanted to stop. I told him I was a Christian, and I did not think it was a good testimony for me to smoke. I took the Winstons out of my pocket and placed them on a parts rack, telling him, "I quit." He reached over and picked them up, saying, "I'm a Christian too, and I'll take them." That was the end of my years of smoking that had started that night when Dennis and I stole them from my dad. I was free from that power over my life.

I was eager to learn all I could about the Bible. As my hunger grew, so did I. I wanted to do more for the Lord, and in time, was asked to teach a third-grade boys class. They didn't have a classroom for me, so I taught them under the baptismal steps. That assignment was a delight to me. I loved the study and the teaching of what I had learned.

23
MY SURRENDER TO GOD

On one Sunday, a missionary to the Philippines was preaching. He was the brother of Florence Friend. The only thing I remember about his sermon was a question. "We watch people go to hell like water over a waterfall, does anyone care?" God was speaking to my heart through that message. I went forward and told the Pastor that I cared and was surrendering my life to God. That day gave meaning and purpose to my life, which I have never forgotten or lost.

One night at work, a Boeing fireman came up to me and said, "I heard that you were a Christian, and I wanted to meet you." That young man was Ray Cazis. Ray and Bonnie became lifetime friends of ours. Like the Friends, they too had two boys about the ages of our sons. At this writing, Ray and Bonnie are serving Christ in Lancaster, California. One of their sons is pastoring in New York.

24

TRANSFER BACK TO SEATTLE

Eventually, the project in Moses Lake ended, and we were back in Seattle. I went to the main plant on Boeing Field, just south of Seattle. We lived in the White Center area in West Seattle. I worked on what is called the graveyard shift. You go to work at twelve midnight and get off at seven a.m. It wasn't long before I understood why they called it the graveyard shift.

Joyce and I found a Bible Baptist Church in the nearby community of Burien. It was a good church, and it wasn't long before we were working with elementary children in a program call King's Kids. It was good training for us, and we enjoyed it.

It was at Bible Baptist we met Roger and Evelyn Hammett. They became dear friends of ours, and after forty-five years, Roger and I stayed in contact. Roger died from mesothelioma cancer and that grieves our hearts, because of the love we had for Roger.

After a few months at the main Boeing plant, I transferred back to the plant in Renton. I worked on side panels. It was an easy job. Everything was out in the open and easy to get to, unlike the wing section or the forty-one section.

It was at this plant I met a dear Christian friend. He and his wife were friends for years. Their names were Harley and Marilyn Lawson. We became the best of friends and shared some fellowship during lunch time. The sad news is that Marilyn died in 2010 with mesothelioma cancer.

Joyce an I had purchased an eight by thirty-six-foot trailer. It was used and was a piece of junk. However, we were young and wanted a home of our own. It was in Kent, Washington, in a rundown trailer court. It was while we were living there that our third son, David, was born. David was brought home in a cardboard nursery box. We placed it on top of the chest of drawers. He slept in it until he outgrew it. We may have lived there a year or so.

25

HELPING BUILD A NEW CHURCH

While attending Bible Baptist Church, we heard that a pastor wanted to start a church in the community of Tukwila. Tukwila was about five miles north of Kent, and we were excited to be part of a new ministry.

Pastor Larry Pollock located a piece of property on the Macadam Road in Tukwila. Two houses and a machine shop were on the two acres. We went to work converting the shop into a small church facility. It took a lot of paint and hard work, but we completed the task. Pastor Pollock purchased some folding chairs and song books. Now, all we needed were people. In time, they came.

I don't know how the arrangements were made, but we moved into the larger house on the church property. The joy of having a house that was large enough for two people to move at the same time and a place for the boys to play was an exciting prospect. There was just one problem; we owned a trailer that we needed to sell. We would have to sell it before we could move. By the grace of God, I found a young man at Boeing who was willing to take over the remaining payments. We signed the papers as quickly as possible, and were rid of that nightmare. We were now ready to move to the house in Tukwila.

That house was a great place to live. Pastor Pollock had two children at that time who were about the same ages as two of our boys. They became lifelong friends. Pastor Pollock became a wonderful friend to me and helped me in my spiritual growth. We spent many hours discussing Scripture. He gave me many opportunities to serve in the new church and prayed for me daily.

The commitment that I had made to the Lord in Soap Lake would not go away. I found myself thinking about it more often and talking to God about it on a regular basis. The house had a full basement, and after work, I would go down and kneel on the laundry Joyce had put it there until she had a full load to wash. My son Rocky would often come down and kneel by me as we prayed. The more I prayed, the stronger was the question about attending Bible College.

I discussed my desire to serve the Lord with Pastor Pollock, and he provided me with several catalogs and wise counsel. I had considered going to Denver, Colorado where Harvey Springer was the pastor and president. Eventually, I received a catalog from the Omaha Baptist Bible College. After much prayer, and discussion with Pastor Pollock, Joyce and I decided that was where we would go.

Joyce's brother, Vernon Smithson, and his family were attending Calvary Baptist Church in Everett, Washington. We would get together as often as possible and spend some time visiting. I told him of our decision to go to Omaha, Nebraska to Bible College. He told me of a family in their church who was leaving in the summer to attend the same college. I asked if Joyce and I could meet them. Vernon worked it out, and we met with Tom and Beth Peace, who are still among our best friends. They left for college a month or so ahead of us. They reminded us of how unbearable the heat was in

Omaha. Thanks to my brother-in-law, Vernon, we still have contact with Tom and Beth.

26
TRANSFER BACK TO SEATTLE - AGAIN

The summer of 1964, I built a trailer to haul our valuables(?). When we loaded the trailer, it was full, when we arrived in Omaha, most of the belongings had settled to the half full mark. We owned a 55 Dodge, that I called Jezebel. However, she got us there with our valuables.

We had a little over $300.00 in a cashier's check. I parked the car in front of the bank to go inside. A lady was standing at the parking meter. When I got out to put money in the meter, she spoke and gave me a gospel tract. I told her I was a Christian and was in town to go to Bible College. I explained that I was going to the bank to cash the check, and then search for an apartment. She smiled and said she knew where an empty apartment was. We followed her to the location, where we lived for the three years in Omaha. God was leading all the way!

Tom and Beth were living in the trailer they had brought from Seattle and were also searching for a place to live. There happened to be another empty apartment in the same building, so they moved in and became our neighbors.

The next order of business was to locate a job. I worked at three different jobs while in Omaha. One was at a frozen food factory. I cannot remember how long I stayed at each job. Another place I worked was at Vickers Machine Shop. My job was to operate a tracing mill. It was there that I met a young man who became one of my best friends. Gene Springer was an inspector. Gene is now pastoring the Open Door Baptist Church in Council Bluff, Iowa, where he has been for over 43 years. He has built a great church, and I am glad to call him my friend. However, I just received word that Gene had major heart surgery and is in rehab. I enjoyed the job at the machine shop, but eventually I heard of a place where I could earn a better salary.

That fall of 1964, I enrolled in Omaha Baptist College. Freshmen were required to take entrance exams. I failed the English test. I am embarrassed to say, at age 25 I did not know how to diagram a sentence, say the multiplication tables, and work on division or fractions. Over the years, I have reaped the results of my lack of education. However, I scored higher than all other students on the Bible exam. I enjoyed college and the learning experiences.

27
HOW GOD PREPARED
ME TO PASTOR

Iowa and Nebraska have hundreds of small farm towns. Most of the churches in these towns are too small to afford a full-time pastor. These small churches contacted the College about students who were capable of filling the pulpits on Sundays. The invitations provided an opportunity for me to preach and gain some pastoral experience. I was asked to preach somewhere almost every Sunday. Little did I realize that God was preparing me for a greater ministry.

I was invited to preach at a small church in Manning, Iowa. The farming town is about seventy miles northeast of Omaha. It was the beginning of summer, and the deacons asked me if I would be willing to pastor the church. I was flattered, and more than willing to do it. The small congregation had purchased an old Lutheran church. A parsonage was next to the church, and we were invited to live there while pastoring. Pastoring was a great learning experience for Joyce and me, and we loved the people, and the opportunity to serve in Manning.

While pastoring at Manning, I attended a Pastors School at the First Baptist Church in Hammond, Indiana. Dr. Jack Hyles was the pastor and the church had several thousand members. I received a phone call from Joyce, who told me she had a surprise for me. We had three boys; I wasn't sure I was ready for another surprise.

However, it was good news. Mr. Sorensen, one of the deacons, was a farmer. He had sold a load of corn and given the check to Joyce so we could purchase a new car. We will never forget the kindness of the people at Manning, Iowa. I am thankful to be a friend on Facebook with one of his daughters.

That fall I was back in class. The Church at Manning asked if I could continue to come over on the weekends to teach and preach. We were welcome to stay in the parsonage Friday and Saturday nights. We continued to preach for them and drove back to Omaha after the services on Sunday night so that we could be ready for class next morning.

Each Friday afternoon, we would load up and drive to Manning for the weekend. About half way to Manning, there was a small drive-in on the left side of the highway. A large ice-cream cone sign extended for display. Our boys learned to watch for it. It became a routine stop for us. David was about three at the time. He would stand in the front seat watching for the sign. When he saw it, he would say, "I want a cone." So did I, so we stopped as usual.

Tom Peace and I needed a job. We had heard that Union Packing Co. had hired many of the college students. The packing company was a slaughter house where beef was killed and processed. They worked six days a week and had two ten hour shifts. Tom and I inquired about a job. We told the foreman that we were students, and physically could not work the hours and attend classes. Then we asked him if he would be willing to hire the two of us as one man. Tom and I would rotate our shifts, to ensure that we did the job. To our surprise, he agreed, on one condition. He assured us he would fire us if one failed to show for work. I must say, although the pay was excellent, I have never had a more difficult job than I had at Union Packing Co. The work was hard, but the pay was good.

While filling out the application in the lunch room, one could look down and see the process from beginning to end. The first step was to bring the cow in, shoot it, shackle it to a hoist and cut its throat. That area was called the blood pit. I noticed that the man working there was eating a candy bar and drinking a cup of coffee. I wondered how he had the stomach to do that. Before long, I found out. I too was working the pit. The job worked out just right for Tom and me.

Tom was interested in becoming an aviation missionary. Beth was interested in becoming a registered nurse. They accomplished both objectives. They were missionaries in Brazil for twenty-nine years on the Amazon River. Tom had to take many hours of flight training. Often he would ask me, Rocky and Randy, if we would love to go along. We were eager to go. There were some unforgettable experiences flying with Tom.

28
A CHANGE OF COLLEGES

The college in Omaha had acquired a large piece of land in Ankeny, Iowa, and was planning to start next fall's classes there. I was becoming discontent with some of the practices of the college and was also planning a transfer to another college. I was considering Baptist Bible College in Springfield, Mo. However, my pastor, Dick Meyer, strongly suggested that I go to Pontiac, Michigan and attend Midwestern Baptist College. His wife was from that area, so we followed the advice of our pastor, and moved to Pontiac that summer. Again, I firmly believe God was in that decision. It was Pastor Meyer who gave me a license to preach when I was a third-year student, and the license meant much to me.

When we arrived in Pontiac, the first place we went was to the college campus. We ask about a place to live and work. A house was available in Union Lake. The house was just right; so we paid the rent and moved in. Pontiac Motors hired many students. I went to the Fisher Body plant, filled out an application, and was hired that week to work the night shift.

After taking care of the house and job matters, we went to the college to register for our classes. It was there we met Stan and Jaxine Blake. They had arrived from Albuquerque and were there to enroll and look for a place to stay. Joyce and I introduced ourselves, and ask them to stay with us until they found a house. They were with us only a few days, and Stan had a house and a job. Everything was now in order, and we were ready for our classes.

Dr. Tom Malone was the president of the college and pastor of Emmanuel Baptist Church. The college had between three and four hundred students, and the church had between two and three thousand members. Dr. Malone was one of the best preachers I have ever heard. What a privilege it was to sit under his ministry.

Attending the College was beyond great; it was one of life's greatest experiences. Most of our teachers were pastoring churches in the area. Therefore, their teaching was not textbook education only, but also practical lessons from their pastoral experiences.

At Midwestern, Joyce and I made many friends. I will not attempt to name them, for fear of leaving someone out. The names of others, I can't remember. We have attempted to stay in contact with many of them over the years.

Emmanuel Baptist also had a Christian school where we enrolled Rocky and Randy. I drove one of the school buses to pay their tuition. On the weekends I would preach at the jail or rest home. Soul winning was required, so I usually went on Saturdays, and Joyce would go with the ladies on Monday evenings. So with the classes, the work, the soul winning and driving the bus to school each day, there was little time left for a social life or family.

Although I enjoyed my time at Midwestern, the work, and school demands took its toll on some families. One of my greatest regrets in life is the little time I took for my family during those years. I am ashamed to say, but I feel that those years my family was blocked out and ignored too much by me. My third son, David, was about three years old when we went to Pontiac. I have little memory of him or the other two boys during that time. Our fourth son, Stephen, was born the third month after we arrived in Pontiac. I have attempted to teach young preachers that they should never allow the work of the ministry or college to rob them of time with their family, no matter how much you enjoy your work. You will regret it.

Before I was allowed to graduate, I was required to pass a GED test. It was also necessary for me to attend summer school to graduate with the class of 1969. I graduated with a Masters of Religious Education. At the time of this writing, I also have a Doctor of Divinity, a Masters of Biblical Studies, a Doctor of Theological Studies, and a Doctor of Ministries.

29

GOD WORKS IN MYSTERIOUS WAYS

As the graduation date drew near, the seniors began to talk about where they were going, and what they were going to do after graduation. Some already had jobs as assistants, others were already pastoring. One student asked me, "Ken, what are you are planning to do?" I told him I didn't have a clue. He said, "Don't they need churches in Washington, why not go and start one?" Those words stuck in my mind, so during summer, Joyce and I begin to pray about that matter. I have no idea who that young man was, but he planted the seed that birthed Open Door Baptist Church. You just never know the impact what you say will have.

I wrote a letter to Harley Lawson, my Boeing friend, asking him to send a map of the Seattle area. After much prayer, Joyce and I concluded that the Lord would have us go north of Seattle, to the Lynnwood, Washington area. We rented a small block house in Mountlake Terrace, and a new phase of our life began.

I was shopping in a hardware store and met a lady that I had known as a teenager. In fact, she married one of my friends, John Fortune, whom I have already mentioned. After being acquainted again, she asked what I was doing. I told her that Joyce and I were going to start a church in Mountlake Terrace. She told me that she and John had accepted Jesus as their Savior under the preaching of

Evangelist Tom Williams. We exchanged phone numbers, said we would be in touch, and went on our way. Her husband helped us financially for the first year with a gift of $100.00 each month. I thank God for the continued friendship we have with the Fortunes even today.

30
THE BIRTH OF OUR CHURCH

I purchased 25 folding metal chairs and 25 songbooks. We set a date for the first service. It would be in our living room. Joyce and I printed invitations with the time and place for the first service. We did not have a computer or electric typewriter. The stencils were a soft felt substance. Joyce placed it in the typewriter, and the keys would cut through the stencil. The mimeograph machine had a drum filled with paste ink from a tube. You placed the stencil over the drum, and you cranking out the flyers or bulletins. Rocky and Randy would go with me throughout the community passing them out or leaving them on the doors. When the date for the first service came, we set up the chairs and laid out the songbook. No one showed up for that first service! Needless to say, I was disappointed.

We advertised a Sunday evening service also. To our surprise, a lady by the name of Jean Wake, who had recently moved from Wenatchee, attended the evening service. She became our piano player, Sunday school teacher, and a large financial contributor to the new church. She and her daughters were members for several years. Not only was Jean a faithful soul winner, but she also became our personal friend.

While attempting to hold services in our home, I began to search for a more acceptable meeting place. The Forest Crest Community Club building was near, and we were able to rent it. It was small but much more practical than our living room. We had some great services in that small building. When we arrived Sunday morning, we had to open doors and windows to ventilate the smell of cigarette smoke and beer left over from Saturday night parties held in the building. Some who accepted Christ at that building are now serving in the ministry in a full-time capacity. It was exciting to see God's blessing on our efforts.

31
MIRACLES AT MOUNTLAKE TERRACE

There is a special day I shall always remember when I was going door to door inviting people to our new church. The first family to show any interest was a gentleman by the name of Tony Geraldo. He invited me in, and I was able to pray with him to accept Christ. He and his family attended Open Door for several years. They were faithful members and workers in the ministry.

A few doors away, a lady by the name of Irene Head came to the door. I remember inviting her to attend services the next Sunday. To my surprise, Irene, her husband Clem, and their seven children showed up for church. That was the beginning of some of the greatest blessings during my thirty-nine years at Open Door. History is still being made as a result of that one family! Several of their children are faithfully serving Christ. Kim Head became one of our best bus captains, and teachers. She later graduated from Hyles-Anderson College and is now faithfully serving in a church in Oregon. Her son is serving on staff, in the music ministry, at Open Door Baptist Church, at this writing.

After visiting at the door with Irene, I continued on to knock on another door nearby. A family I will never forget is Carol and Jim Violanti. Carol came to the door. I spoke briefly with her and asked if I could show her from the Bible how to be sure of heaven. She said she was putting her baby to bed, and asked if I could come back in thirty minutes. Within thirty minutes I was back at her home. She invited me in, and again I explained my purpose. After showing her from the Bible how to be saved, we knelt and she accepted Christ as her Savior. She and Jim were in our church for years, and she became one of the most faithful teachers we have ever had.

After a few weeks, Clem and Irene Head invited several of their nieces and nephews to church. I believe there were six or seven brothers and sisters from one family. They were from the Backstrom family, and if my memory is right, Raydine, the oldest girl was the first to trust Christ. Mrs. Blue prayed with her. Each week one of the Backstroms would come forward to trust Christ. Praise God!

Sherri was a beautiful blond, about sixteen years of age. I remember well the morning she accepted Christ as her Savior. She told me that the young man she was dating was not saved. She wanted me to talk with him. We set a date and time for them to come to our home. After the introduction and some small talk, I spoke to him about being saved. We knelt and prayed as he received Christ. That young man is Pat Stevens. Pat went to Bible College and returned to be on our staff. Not only did I marry them, but Pat and Sherri have also pastored Lake Country Baptist Church for 28 years in Lake Stevens, Washington. They have a great church and a wonderful family.

When the time came for Pat and Sherri to be married, they asked me to do the service. I had never performed a wedding. Thus, I had no idea what I was doing. I do remember that it was an outside wedding. The weather was perfect. The chairs were in place. An arch draped with beautiful flowers made a perfect setting. The Bride and her maids were beautiful. They had planned every detail, including the special music. I followed a wedding outline someone had given me. Everyone was in place, and I proceeded through my outline. I had no idea that special music was planned, so I just plowed through my outline. I found out later; there were some unhappy people. I guess it was ok. They will have been married 45 years August 2017.

God also gave me the privilege of marrying Sherrie's older sister, Raydine to a young man in our church by the name of Roger Hudson. They are still serving the Lord in a Church in Brier, Washington that is pastored by their two sons. Another sister, Laurie, was married by me to my son Randy. They pastored in Mount Vernon, Washington, fourteen years. A brother, Kelly was saved in our church and worked for me several years. I married him to a young lady in our church named Jan Argento. Kelly and Jan pastored in Vancouver, WA. Another sister, Becky, met Richard Szydlowski in Bible College. I married them also. Richard and Becky worked for me a few years. They are presently pastoring in Banning, California and doing an outstanding job.

The above demonstrates just what one family, Clem and Irene Head, accomplished for the glory of God, and that is only the beginning of a wonderful story. Their story would be a blockbuster, should one of them choose to write it. I hope they will. I can truthfully say that I love the Heads and the Backstroms as my own family.

Another young man, Steve Hicks, attended Bob Jones University. He returned to Open Door. In a brief time he was called to pastor Lincoln Park Baptist Church in Wenatchee, Washington. I believe Steve was there about twenty years. He is now pastoring in the Kent/Renton area. Of the many outstanding qualities Steve possessed, faithfulness to the Lord stands out most. Steve's parents still attend Open Door Baptist in Lynnwood. His mother has faithfully worked in the nursery for many years, and his dad did all our printing for years.

32
THE BIRTH OF OUR DAUGHTER

I had graduated in 1969 and was thirty years old. We started Open Door Baptist Church that fall in the month of October. Our daughter, Lisa was born June 15, 1970, while we were in Mountlake Terrace. Neither Joyce nor I were too excited about this pregnancy. Joyce was deathly sick at the sight or smell of food, and I wasn't too thrilled about another boy.

33
MY BOUT WITH CANCER

In May of the following year, I began to have some digestive problems. At first, I thought I was constipated. I would eat a few bites and then felt the urge to go to the bathroom. I would strain, and a small stool would ribbon out. It was on a Saturday afternoon that I told Joyce I felt sick to my stomach. She suggested I should go to the doctor the next Monday.

My third son, David, was attending King's Garden Christian School in Edmonds. His teacher, Mrs. Staatz, and her family were members of our church. She told my wife of their family doctor. His name was Kyle Chapman. On Tuesday morning I had an appointment to see him. After the examination, he said, "I don't have good news for you. You have cancer of the colon and total blockage." I told him that I did not have any insurance. He said, "We can't be concerned about that now. We should plan for surgery this Friday." Thankfully, he was the cancer specialist in the Seattle area. Another note of praise was, I never received a bill for the surgery or the hospital, or for any other service.

Needless to say, my wife and I were in shock and disbelief at the news that I had cancer. I was only thirty-one years old; we had four young boys and an infant daughter. Had we attended five years of Bible College, and come this far to see it end in an early death? As I said earlier, our family was plagued with cancer on my mother's side.

In addition, my best friend and first cousin, Johnny Byler, died of cancer at the same time I had cancer. He was just thirty-four when he died. Those were some dark days for Johnny's family, and our own as well. Thankfully, Johnny was a dedicated Christian. I look forward to seeing him in heaven.

Three pastor friends came to our house to pray for me when they heard I had cancer. Their names are Dwayne Wells, Ron McGaughey, and Mark Luthole. These men lay on the floor with their arms around my feet, praying and begging God to spare my life. God heard their prayers, and has given me forty-four additional years, plus, to serve Him! Glory to His name!

After the operation, the doctor informed my wife that he had to remove eighteen inches of my colon. The cancer had grown through the colon wall, so a large dose of radiation was injected to kill any seeds that might have missed. By God's grace, I have been cancer free all these years. In addition, that experience has opened the door for me to minister to many who had cancer.

34
PASTORS WHO IMPACTED OUR LIFE

Joyce and I discovered two small Baptist Churches nearby. One was about a mile south and was pastored by Pastor Don Beene. The other was about three miles north and was pastored by Pastor Ron McGaughey. We became good friends with both pastors and their families. It was not uncommon to meet with them at a nearby restaurant on Sunday evening after church for a bite to eat, and fellowship. Although their churches were small, they had big hearts and opened them to us.

My last conversation with Brother Beene was on a Saturday morning at Denny's in Lynnwood. I remember Don telling me about the weakness that he experienced while working underneath his car the day before. I gave that comment little attention until later. That week Don experienced a massive stroke at work and never recovered. He lived for another year in a nursing home, where he died at age thirty-nine. Don's wife, Mary, became a member of Open Door after his death. She has attended Open Door for over 35 years and is a special friend of ours.

I sometimes marvel at how some people manage to deal with life's aches. After the death of Don, Mary started attending our church. After a few years, she remarried, however, that ended in a divorce. Her oldest daughter, Dianne, had a baby girl that lived with cancer for four years before she died at age twelve. Within a year, Dianne, the mother died also. In August 2012 Mary's only son, Mark also died. Mary has one living daughter. Her name is Kim. Joyce and I love Mary and Kim very much. They are like family to us.

The other Pastor, Ron McGaughey, also suffered from health problems and felt he was unable to take his small church forward. He had located three acres of prime property on 44th Ave. in Lynnwood. We met at the property, and he explained that his church was not able to purchase it, and believed it would be a great location for us.

35

THE PURCHASE OF
PROPERTY ON 44TH AVE.

A few days later I took our church members to look at the property. We walked around, looking it over, had a word of prayer and later decided we would make an offer. The price was $55,000.00 we had $5,000.00 in the bank. I called the owner and discussed our plans. I told her we had $5,000.00 to put down and asked if she would carry the contract. She agreed to all the terms, and we made the purchase. Today, beautiful church buildings are on that site, and the church is debt free.

The property was north of the Lynnwood city limits at that time. The previous owners had a commercial egg business on the property years earlier. They had started building a beautiful home with a full basement. The tile roof, rough plumbing, framing, and outside press-board had been installed. Something happened, and the owners got a divorce. The chicken houses and the new home were not completed. The property was neglected for years. However, its location on 44th Ave. was a perfect location.

I never saw a more enthusiastic group of people than our church members. They had a vision, and a mind to work. We hired an engineer to draw up the plans and get a permit for the completion of the building. In a few months, the house was renovated into a wonderful meeting place. A church in Wenatchee gave us some old hardwood pews. We painted them dark brown, and they were as good as new. Thanks to the hard work of our members, we were able to have our first service on our property in October of 1972.

Brother Gene Springer, the young inspector I met in Omaha, had graduated from Midwestern Bible College and agreed to come to Washington to work with us. He served as youth pastor and was in charge of the bus ministry, and was a great help in foundational part of the church. One of the children he contacted through bus visitation is now a grown man with his family in the church. His family, the Halls, continue to serve at Open Door. Gene Springer was one of the best staff members I ever had. He was loyal, dependable, and loved the Lord. He later returned to Council Bluffs, Iowa and started the Open Door Baptist Church. He has remained at the church for forty-four years and has done a wonderful job. At this writing, they came to visit us. Thank God for the tender heart of Brother Springer and his wife.

I might add that the Hall family had special friends named Jerry and Kathy Lundquist. The Halls wanted them saved and asked if I could make an unexpected call at their house on a set date. They would have Jerry there, and I would just stop by "unexpectedly". Therefore, the plot was laid. I knocked on the door, and was greeted by the Hall family. I saw they had company, and suggested I come some other time. "No, no," they said. "We want you to meet our friend." I went in and introduced myself to Jerry. They were sitting at the table, so I joined them. Within thirty minutes Jerry had accepted Christ. Jerry and Kathy became members of Open Door, and they were two of the most faithful and hard-working members of the church.

36
THE GROWTH OF
OPEN DOOR BAPTIST CHURCH

Evangelist Bob Eaton was our first guest speaker, and we had special services each night. Steve and Sharon Hakala were members of our church and were from Sand Point, Alaska. Sharon's parents were visiting and attended each night. On Friday night, Sharon's dad, Emil Gunderson, accepted Christ as his Savior! What a time of rejoicing we had.

In addition, his salvation opened the door for me to visit Sand Point later and preach a week of meetings. We had a total of forty-one professions of faith! It was never seen before or since like that in the islands. We made many friends at Sand Point, and we are still in contact with some of them. That experience was one of the highlights of my life. It began with Bob Eaton and the Hakala family.

We were purchasing buses as fast as finances would allow. I believe at the time we had five or six buses. It was not uncommon for each bus to have fifty to one hundred on a bus. It was just a matter of time before we outgrew the converted house, and were desperate for additional space. We located two module buildings that had belonged to a public school. I think they gave them to us, at no charge just to take them away. Each building had two rooms. That gave us four additional classrooms. We also had classes on church buses and wherever we could find ample space.

Since we had a large bus ministry, I contacted the best bus pastor in the country. Dr. Jim Vineyard was on staff at First Baptist Church in Hammond, Indiana, where Dr. Jack Hyles pastored. Brother Vineyard came and created a vision on how to reach more boys and girls for Christ. I believe that was in the spring of 1973.

Eventually, we ran out of room for additional growth. It was evident that a new building was needed. We measured for building dimensions and began plans for a new structure. The building department would not allow us to join the two together. The new building was one hundred feet long, and seventy-seven feet wide. It would be two stories with a balcony. Plans were drawn and submitted for a building permit. The permit was granted, and we began this major building project. We did not borrow money, nor did we hire a contractor to build.

The fact that we were doing all the work did not set well with the local union or the building department. Thus, they fought us all the way. I hired an attorney to fight our battles, and he was a pit bull. He did not stop the harassment, but he slowed it a bit. We were breaking no laws and had every right to build. It was the masonry and the steel unions who pressured the building department to stop us. They did not, nor could they.

As stated, the new building would be seventy-seven feet wide. The walls were of masonry blocks and filled with steel rebar and cement. The trusses had to span that distance and support the roof. We ordered the required timbers and steel plates to build the trusses. These were built by our men in the church parking lot. We later hired a crane operator to come and set the trusses in place. It was quite a sight to see these huge trusses in the air and put in place.

God had blessed us with several carpenters, welders, and a professional builder who was an expert at laying the masonry blocks. Also, Brian Bennett was a great addition to our team. He was strong and capable for any task. We had all the helpers we needed, and the people had a mind to work. Thus, the first story was built, and we used it as space permitted. God continued to bless our work and efforts.

The church continued to grow, and about a year later we added the second story which became the main auditorium. It would seat about seven hundred people and was filled many times. Each Sunday we saw people make professions of faith, and others surrender their life for God's service. Thus, the new building provided the space needed for the new growth, which God gave.

However, in time additional space was needed for classrooms. So, another building project was underway. The new building is one hundred and twenty feet long and fifty feet wide. It is a two story building. Again, our people did all the work. We never borrowed money during my thirty-nine years as pastor.

Over the years God gave me some wonderful staff members. Brother Al Hughes finished college about three years after me. He called and said he wanted to come to Washington to start a church. We were eager to help in any way possible. He located in Redmond, Washington, and labored there about two years. Sadly, things did not go has expected. We talked, and he agreed to come on staff at Open

Door. He served three years, and then received a call to come to Barton, Vermont to help start a new church. He moved there and had great success. However, in time, a rich church member began to give him problems. He called me, and I invited him to come back on staff. After five years, he was asked to pastor a church in Port Orchard, WA. He has been there over 31 years and has done a magnificent job. Pastor Al Hughes was a great addition to our ministry.

The present pastor at Open Door, Jason Murphy, served as an assistant for six years until I resigned due to ALS. He was voted to take the senior pastor position when I resigned.

Jason's parents were won to Christ by Jean Wake when our church was in its third year. They were faithful for many years. They have two sons who attended church with them. Both sons are in the ministry serving the Lord. Their mother went home to be with the Lord a few years ago.

We had many guest speakers over the years. Dr. Tom Malone was one of them. Dr. Malone was founder and pastor of Emmanuel Baptist in Pontiac, MI. He was also president of Midwestern Baptist College where I was graduated. A year later his son came and preached for us. When he saw the work we were doing, he called his father and recommended that the college give me an honorary doctor's degree. I must say that I was flattered that they were so impressed with the work God was doing. I appreciate their bestowal of the Doctorate of Divinity upon me.

While meeting on the ground level of our new building, we invited another guest speaker. The first was Dr. Bob Gray. We had not built a platform yet. Therefore, we stacked wooden pallets and put carpet over them. They worked just fine. The following year we had Dr. Gray and Dr. Dallas Dobson. Brother Dobson was a pastor in Pasco, WA. This time we had a platform in place. The fellowship was great, and the people were wonderful to us. Dr. Dobson died a few years later of kidney cancer.

Dr. Dobson became one of my dear friends. We traveled to Korea together with Dr. Ray Batama, and Dr. Jerry Prevo. Larry Chappell was a missionary in Korea at that time. That trip also extends to the Philippines, and Hong Kong. On our return flight home, I was seated next to Dr. Prevo who pastored in Anchorage, Alaska. He asked if Joyce and I had ever been to Hawaii. I told him we had not. He said he and his wife Carol were going for a week and that they would be gone for the weekend; would I be willing to come and preach that weekend, and then join them in Hawaii the following Monday. "We will take care of all expenses." How could I turn down an offer like that? Of course we would love to do that. Dr. Prevo became my dear friend. I preached for him on several occasions.

Dr. Ray Batama also became a dear friend. He was one of the best preachers I've ever heard, other than Dr. Malone. Brother Batama pastored a beautiful church by the freeway in Pomona, CA. We had him at Open Door on many occasions.

We also had Dr. Jack Hyles on many occasions. Dr. Curtis Hutson, Dr. Jim Modlish, Dr. Ken Bates, Dr. Dave Reese, Dr. Herb

Noe and Dr. Peter Ruckman Dr. John Rawlins and many others whose names I can't remember. Our people were exposed to the best.

Dr. Paul Vanaman was one of my professors at college. When he heard that I had cancer, he sent a check for a few hundred dollars. He said it was for us, and if we gave it to the church, he would get me for embezzling funds. In addition, missionary, Colin Christian, sent $25.00 each month for a year. I attended college with him. He recently died of cancer.

Dr. Vanaman called me a few years after we founded the church and invited Joyce and me to take a trip with him and others to Israel. A few years later he invited us to take another trip. This time we went to Lucerne, Switzerland, Liechtenstein, and Germany. We traveled through these countries by bus. We return to Lucerne, from where we flew to Ammon, Jordan. While in Jordan, we rented horses and guides and visited the hidden city of Petra. That was one of the highlights of our trip. One must see it to believe it.

From Jordan, we rode a bus to Israel and entered Israel at the Allenby Bridge. We spent about seven days in Israel. We visited the Dead Sea, took the tramway up to Masada, visited the site of Jesus' tomb, visited Bethlehem city, the city of Nazareth, the tomb of Lazarus, and took a boat ride across the Sea of Galilee. We also visited the Golan Heights and viewed the valley where the Battle of Armageddon will be fought.

From Israel, we took a bus tour of Egypt. We were able to ride camels and visit the pyramids. Tours were provided to go inside the pyramid. I was eager to go. Joyce was not. She remained outside until we returned. Inside the pyramid was a small room with a sarcophagus of granite. Joyce and I also took a ride in a small sailboat on the river Nile. It brought back memories of the fact that baby Moses was at one time on these same waters.

There were other trips to Israel with Pastor Bill Tate, Pastor Al Hughes, and others. First class was empty, so our group was moved up to where the rich people fly. We landed in Copenhagen. From there we flew on to Israel.

Open Door has always had a world vision. From the beginning, we have trained men and women for the mission field. I have discovered that the best way to stir the heart for missions, it to take others to visit the mission field.

Dr. Steve Zeinner was working in Mexico when we began his support. He now has a word ministry of publishing the Scriptures in languages where the people do not have the Word of God.

After traveling with me on a mission trip to India, Brother Mitch Muller was called to the mission field and planted churches in Mexico. He is now working with Hispanics in Southern California with Pastor Tim Shanks.

Open Door was the first church to begin support for Kory Mears who is faithfully serving in Fiji.

Dr. Newell, along with Shane Montgomery and his family, served in Rotorua, New Zealand.

Open Door supported Missionary Dr. John Cook during the many years he served in Canada.

Open Door has supported Dr. Dave Reese and his ministry in the Philippians. Dr. Reese has faithfully served there for many years.

Open Door has also had a major part in a ministry in India. Dr. Joseph Garikapaty, his family, and network of rural village pastors are reaching hundreds for Christ. They run a Christian school, educating and witnessing to village Hindu and Muslim children, who in turn, go home and witness to their families.

Open Door also supported Dr. Larry Chappel and Pastor Leo Dutton in Korea.

37

PROBLEM AREAS IN THE CHURCH

Although God blessed our ministry above and beyond what we could imagine, I don't want to give the impression that we were without problems and challenges.

HARASSMENT BY COUNTY AND CITY

One of the continuing problems was with the Snohomish County building department. I mentioned that earlier. They were determined to make things as difficult as possible. Their first attack was to send, someone to audit our financial transactions, hoping to find some discrepancy. They found nothing. Once the church was incorporated within the Lynnwood city limits, the city took up where the county left off. Each month we would have a visit from the fire department, or the building department, and the environmental department.

On one occasion, we had an evangelist for a week of meetings. He parked his truck and trailer next to the church. That week I had a visit from the "nuisance" Department of Lynnwood. The "hit man" said he had a report that someone was living on the property. I was so upset; I almost threw him out the door. I demanded he tells me who complained. He would not. Kelly Backstrom, my assistant at that time, knew the receptionist at city hall. He called and asked if there had been any complaints about our church. She informed him there was none. We were blessed by having a Lynnwood police officer in our church. I related the story to him. He asks for the "hit man's" card. He said, "The little weasel will tell me who called." He informed me that he had a talk with the "little weasel" from the "nuisance" department. He said he informed him that Open Door was his church, and if he did not back off, he would start investigating him. The harassment stopped.

MORAL PROBLEMS

Another incident involved child molestation. A mother called to inform me that her daughter had confided in her aunt that her stepdad was molesting her. The mother verified the story with her daughter and called the county sheriff, after that, she called me. This was a new experience in my ministry, so I had to "wing" it. On Sunday night I named twelve men that I would like to meet with after the service. I related the story to them and asked their advice. They all said the man had to leave the church. I later met with the stepdad and relayed the verdict. Not only did he leave the church, but his wife also left him. The oldest daughter in the family was his from a previous marriage. She blamed me for breaking up her family. She printed up a letter blaming me for the breakup of her family. She posted the letters on every windshield in the parking lot. Nothing further came of that event.

THE PROBLEM FROM EX-PASTORS

Again, when our church was young, two ex-pastors attending our church, on two different occasions decided they would leave and take their "followers" with them. One started a church with his group. Within one year, the people left him, and he locked the doors. He came to me and asked if he could come back. I allowed him to do so. He never was a problem after that. The main reason I allowed him to return was because of his godly wife. She informed me that she had no idea what he was doing, and was not a part of it. Her record at Open Door gave me no reason to doubt her word.

The other pastor took his group, and they joined another church a few miles away. He disagreed with me over the issue of dispensations. He could not understand or accept the right divisions of Scripture. Therefore, he divided a small group of his workers and left. He was never a problem before that, nor afterward.

THE DEACON THIEF

The biggest surprise came when my wife and the church secretary informed me that someone was taking money from the church offerings. I did not want to believe this, for that meant I had to deal with it. To prove her point, Joyce put one hundred dollars cash in her offering envelope. On Monday morning when the report was generated from the empty envelopes, my wife's envelope was not among them. It was obvious someone in that department was stealing the cash.

We sent our membership a record of their giving every four months. One of our faithful men called to inform me there was a huge discrepancy in his giving report. He said he had given fifty dollars ever week that year, yet only fifty dollars showed on his giving report. He then said, "Pastor, you have a thief in the church." Since we kept all the giving envelopes, I ask him to come to the church office. I had the secretary to go through the envelopes, and only one envelope showed up with his name on it. I looked at the date on the envelope; it just happened to be the very Sunday one of our money counters was on vacation. We now knew who the thief was.

We had four people working in the money counting room at all times. One was a Lynnwood police officer. I discussed the issue with him. He suggested we mount a hidden camera, which we did. Also, we photocopied five one hundred dollar bills and put three in one offering envelope and two in another. We put names of men who regularly gave cash. Those two envelopes were missing when envelopes were counted Monday morning. Envelopes were stolen right under the Officer's nose. Also, we did not have it on tape for some reason.

Next Sunday, we did the same procedure, with the exception that the recording device was on and working. After the money counters had left the room, the Officer went in and checked the stack of empty envelopes, and the two with the money were in the stack unopened. We waited and watched the monitor. Within five minutes, the thief came in, removed the two envelopes from the stack, and put them in his inside coat pocket. I watched from my office window as he went to his car and put his Bible and the two envelopes in the trunk. A police car was waiting nearby, and after the arrest, he was placed into a police car and taken to jail. My advice to every pastor is to have full proof policies and protection in place when it comes to the finances. I can't think of anything more wicked than stealing the money that others had given to God. Was this person saved? I doubt it. Was he possessed of a Devil? Perhaps both.

That night I had to make an announcement of the theft and arrest. Many of our people were shocked beyond belief. Why? Because the man in question appeared to be a "stellar" Christian. So much for spiritual discernment in the Body of Christ.

ANONYMOUS LETTERS, NOT SO ANONYMOUS

Not only was this man a thief, but he had also written several anonymous letters to the membership, accusing me and my family of everything he could think of.

One such letter had photo copies of canceled checks written to me for salary. I was paid monthly, but he made it appear that it was weekly, thus enlarging my salary. Also, at the end of the letter, he typed R. Blue, making is look like it was from my son. In fact, he put that son's return address on the envelope. The letters stopped when he was arrested and removed from the church.

It was also discovered that he was stealing items from where he worked. He was then selling the items wherever he could.

I mention the above to let young pastors know that when God is blessing, the Devil is fighting. When light invades his kingdom of darkness, you can expect opposition. My advice is, don't give up!

38
MY ALS DIAGNOSIS

As mentioned earlier, I injured my back at work in Rock Island, WA. Over these years, the injury has caused me much pain. The pinched nerve sends pain down my right leg to my foot. I have been to many chiropractors, but to no avail. About ten years ago I began to stumble and fall. I was sure it was the result of the back injury, and the only remedy was surgery.

My primary physician sent me to a neurologist for the test. After three months of different doctors and test, they concluded that I had ALS (amyotrophic lateral sclerosis). As I read the symptoms online, I was convinced that they were right in their diagnosis. People who have ALS have an average lifespan of five years. By God's grace, So far, He has given me twice that.

At this writing, I am confined to a wheelchair. I am unable to speak or eat solid foods. I have a feeding tube in my stomach for supplements. I am unable to transfer or turn over in bed without assistance. I'm still able to sit up in the wheelchair, and also use my hands, although they are feeling the effects of ALS and becoming more paralyzed day by day. I thank God for His grace and the prayers of the saints.

Joyce and I had plans, before the diagnoses, to purchase a trailer, travel to small churches, and offer any help we could. I had purchased a new Chevrolet truck, fully equipped, for that purpose. However,

God had different plans for us. God willing, I intend to post my former sermons online and write articles to help others.

I have over 600 sermons on YouTube

I have a blog page at ken@kenblueministries.com

I have a Facebook page

Books and commentaries and CD at Amazon and

https://opendoor.cartloom.com

39
THE FINAL CHAPTER?

In spite of the covert attacks on my family and me, God continued to bless every Sunday with professions of faith by those needing the Savior. In addition, young people surrendered to the Lord for full-time service. Some are pastoring churches; others are on the mission field.

By the grace of God, all our personal needs were met over the years. The ministry is the very place God wanted me. Not only have we witnessed the salvation of hundreds, perhaps thousands, at Open Door, but we have also seen multitudes surrender their life for full-time service for Christ. That continues today under the excellent leadership of Pastor Jason Murphy.

I am so grateful for the hundreds who faithfully pray for Joyce and me. I firmly believe God answers their prayers and supplies His abundant grace. His grace is sufficient.

I thank God that, during this time of trials, I can still use my hands to type, which is something I do each day. Also, on Facebook I can communicate with many friends.

No one but God knows when or how our journey will end. If the Lord tarries, it is certain to end for each of us. Most people with ALS leave this world as the result of pneumonia. Regardless of how God chooses to take me home, it will be wonderful to see Him and touch Him. Pray that my departure will glorify Him.

Finally, I say to you, God's grace is sufficient for any and all trials you will experience. Have no fear. He will never forsake you. Romans eight comes to mind, and I will include it here. *"Who shall separate us from the love of Christ? shall tribulation, or distress, or persecution, or famine, or nakedness, or peril, or sword? As it is written, for thy sake we are killed all the day long; we are accounted as sheep for the slaughter. Nay, in all these things we are more than conquerors through him that loved us. For I am persuaded, that neither death, nor life, nor angels, nor principalities, nor powers, nor things present, nor things to come, Nor height, nor depth, nor any other creature, shall be able to separate us from the love of God, which is in Christ Jesus our Lord."* Romans 8:35-39. Nothing can separate us from Him or His love! Rest in that love.

Life has been more than good to me. No one could have had a more loving mother or extended family. The love of the people at Open Door Baptist Church has helped sustain us. We learned to love them with all our hearts. Pastor and Missionary friends, we have had in abundance. God has knitted our hearts to so many of them. I can say with certainty, there has never been a need that God has not met with an abundant supply. Therefore, it doesn't seem sufficient to say God is good. Not only is He good, but He also gives life more abundant.

In this last paragraph, I want to say some things about my family. I have explained how I met Joyce, the love of my life, and co-laborer in the ministry, regardless of where it took us. Joyce is foremost a wonderful wife and an outstanding mother. Her first concern was always about her family. She has done perfectly what God created her to do. Rocky, our first born, and Randy were the joy of my young manhood. They were different in a good way, but at my young age, I did not always see that. Rocky was more artistic and detailed in his approach to life. A father could not be more proud of a son that I am my son Rocky. I love you son. As I said, Randy was different in his interest and personality. Randy seemed to be a little more interested in books and sports than Rocky. Randy is an excellent reader and has great comprehension. He has leadership ability and is an excellent salesman. I love you Randy, and you have been a joy to my life. David was five years younger than Randy. He was born in Auburn, WA. I was working at Boeing when David was born. I deeply regret that I was absent much of the time he needed me. David is the survivor and can fix anything. He is bright and eager to learn. My love for him knows no bounds. Steve is our fourth son. He was born in Pontiac, Michigan. He was the baby boy for years. Steve had a natural humorous personality. He spent twenty years in the Navy as a Yeoman. He is well educated, organized, and is currently working on his Doctrate in buisness. Our daughter Lisa has been the joy of my life. God was richly blessing us in every way. I loved spoiling her then, and still do today. Lisa has started her own cupcake business in Wenatchee and Leavenworth, WA. She named it Cupcake Blues, and it is very successful. She faithfully worked every position for the Costco Stores for twenty-three years. She has proven to be a real entrepreneur. I am proud of her and her family.

I WISH I'D DONE THAT

My little boy came running in to show me a bug he'd found. But I was too busy with my own affairs just to turn around. I wish I'd done that.

Another son came rushing home to tell of the game and score. But I was busy with other things just like the times before. I wish I'd done that.

I put my little girl in bed, she said, "Daddy, let us pray." I said, "It's getting late sweetheart, tomorrow's a busy day." I wish I'd done that.

I spent five years in Bible College, working both day and night. I had little time for wife or children; or to hold them tight. I wish I'd done that.

My beloved mother said to me, "I love you," every day. I did not respond in kind to her, and now she's gone away. I wish I'd done that.

There are many pilgrims struggling along on life's rocky road. I could have shared a helpful hand, lightening their heavy load. I wish I'd done that.

A man asked me of salvation and what it was all about. "I must rush to a meeting; I'll find someone to help you out." I wish I'd done that.

Its judgment time for me now, I find much wood, stubble, and hay. The opportunities that I had are burned and drift away. I wish I'd done that.

And now I say, to friends and family as we approach the line, I love you, and I wanted to tell you while there was still time. I'm glad I did that.

My favorite Bible verse: *"But God commendeth his love toward us, in that, while we were yet sinners, Christ died for us."* Romans 5:8.

"The grace of the Lord Jesus Christ, and the love of God, and the communion of the Holy Ghost, be with you all. Amen."
II Corinthians 13:14.

Photographs

Me as a baby

Cheston Davis –*my biological father*

Grandpa Byler and me

Dennis Britt –*best friend*

Our house on Uncle John Byler's property
(Notice the foundation)

Johnny Wayne, Jimmy Dale, and me

One room school –*Boswell, Arkansas*

Mom and me *–my first love*

Piney Creek *–where I learned to swim*

Lt. Col. Oliver L. North and me

Future home of Open Door Baptist Church, 1972

Open Door Baptist Church –*present day*